TANTRAYUKTI

INDICA

TANTRAYUKTI

IKS-based Handbook for Thesis construction

PROF. M. JAYARAMAN

INDICA

Published by Indica

ISBN 978-1-970452-00-6

Contents

Preface

In the past decade, Indian Knowledge Systems (IKS) have emerged as a critical area of focus in academia, with significant support from institutions such as the All-India Council for Technical Education (AICTE) and the University Grants Commission (UGC). These bodies have increasingly recognized the value of IKS, integrating it into curricula and encouraging research in this field. Even premier institutions like the Indian Institutes of Technology (IITs) have joined the fray, establishing IKS divisions within their campuses to foster interdisciplinary research and innovation rooted in traditional knowledge. The resurgence in interest has acquired momentum with the advent of New Education Policy 2020. National Education policy, 2020 states the following (4.27, p.16) with regard to IKS -

"Knowledge of India" will include knowledge from ancient India and its contributions to modern India and its successes and challenges, and a clear sense of India's future aspirations with regard to education, health, environment, etc. These elements will be incorporated in an accurate and scientific manner..."

To achieve the accurate and scientific incorporation of IKS-related wisdom into educational curricula, it is crucial to understand the methodologies through which these texts were constructed. This includes examining the systematic frameworks and structures inherent in them. Understanding Tantrayuktis—the text construction methodology of Indian Knowledge Systems and the subject matter of this book—is essential for this purpose.

It is important to note that Malaviya Mission Teacher Training Program of UGC (for training of teachers in Higher Education Institutions of India) under the list of its programs includes Indian Knowledge Systems. Further under IKS – as sub theme IV – Tantrayuktis is mentioned (Refer: https://mmc.ugc.ac.in/Home/Indian_Knowledge_System)

What is Tantrayuktis? While the Upaniṣadic dialogues exemplify the ideal of systematic oral expression of knowledge, Tantrayuktis, discussed in the texts of the yore, establish the norms for systematic text construction. This book is a humble effort to introduce Tantrayuktis in an accessible and practical manner, particularly for endeavors related to the study and application of IKS.

Another key question is whether traditional textual methodologies like Tantrayuktis can be adapted for structuring IKS-based research theses. Exploring how these ancient approaches to knowledge construction can enrich contemporary research methodologies is vital for bridging traditional wisdom with contemporary academic inquiry. This book delves into the application of Tantrayuktis in thesis construction with detailed discussions.

In 2009, I submitted my thesis to the University of Madras, which explored Tantrayuktis as a pan-Indian text construction methodology, specifically focusing on Tantrayuktis of Kauṭilya's Arthaśāstra and Tolkāppiyam of Tamil literature. Since then, I have been actively involved in academic pursuits disseminating this approach. Through my academic journey, I have continued to delve into the nuances of Tantrayuktis, aiming to foster understanding of its applications in research methodology for Indian Knowledge Systems (IKS). This book is the culmination of over a decade of exploration and engagement with Tantrayuktis. It draws upon insights gained from numerous lectures, workshops, and interactions with scholars, students, and professionals from diverse backgrounds.

It is noteworthy that this is not the first independent study on Tantrayukti. In the 9th century CE, Nīlamegha Bhaiṣajaka authored a text titled

Tantrayukti Vicāra, where he identified and described 36 Tantrayuktis as applicable to Āyurveda. More recently, Prof. W.K. Lele (1981) brought renewed attention to Tantrayukti, emphasizing its relevance across all Indian Knowledge Systems (IKS). He revised and expanded his work in 2007. (More details in this regard can be seen in Chapter 2 – Tantrayukti through Ages)

However, Prof. Lele's contributions, while groundbreaking, leave certain gaps. Although he explained the yuktis, he did not adequately illustrate them, nor does his work explore the role of tantrayuktis in shaping the content, structure, and language of systematic works within IKS or other related domains.

This work aims to address these shortcomings by offering deeper insights into the practical application of tantrayuktis. It seeks to bridge theoretical understanding with concrete examples, thereby enhancing their utility in the study and development of Indian Knowledge Systems.

The journey in this book is begun with an exploration of Tantrayuktis as a gateway to traditional methodologies in Chapter 1. The definitions, etymology, the list of Tantrayuktis, and associated devices are introduced in this section. This foundational understanding establishes the significance of Tantrayuktis as a vital intellectual tool in the Indian knowledge systems.

The second chapter of this book, Tantrayuktis Through the Ages, explores the evolution of Tantrayuktis in India's intellectual heritage. Tantrayuktis is recognized as a cornerstone of text construction methodology in Ancient Bhārata, evident in works such as Kauṭilya's Arthaśāstra, Caraka-saṃhitā, and suśruta-saṃhitā. Similarly, the Tamil tradition, starting with the Tolkāppiyam, also demonstrates the use of Tantrayuktis in text construction. Traces of Tantrayuktis can also be found in the Pāli tradition. These aspects are discussed in this chapter.

The third chapter of this book explores the *Functional Dynamics of Tantrayuktis*, examining its roles and applications as referenced in the aforementioned classical texts, as well as in the works of later scholars.

The fourth chapter of this book, which is the heart of the work, focuses on the *Devices of Tantrayuktis*, examining both their theoretical foundations and practical applications. Each of the 32 Tantrayuktis from Kauṭilya's Arthaśāstra is analyzed, beginning with clear definitions from the text. These definitions are then illustrated through examples drawn from various Indian Knowledge Systems (IKS) texts, including Kauṭilya's Arthaśāstra, the Caraka-saṃhitā, the Suśruta-saṃhitā, Śri Śaṅkarācārya's commentaries on the Bhagavadgītā and Brahmasūtras, the Aṣṭādhyāyī of Pāṇini, and the Yogasūtras of Sage Patañjali. These examples highlight the broad applicability of Tantrayuktis across different disciplines, including both the humanities and the sciences. In addition to definitions and examples, the chapter includes notes and observations that enhance understanding of each Tantrayuktis. Key takeaways for researchers involved in thesis construction, as well as for evaluators of theses, are provided at the end of each section. The chapter also features activities such as self-reflection questions, critical thinking exercises, and suggestions for applying Tantrayuktis in practical thesis construction scenarios, encouraging a more hands-on approach to learning and application.

The fifth chapter in the book emphasizes the *Integration of Tantrayuktis in the thesis review process* and grading, providing a structured approach to ensure the quality and coherence of academic research.

The penultimate chapter - *Excellences and Pitfalls in Thesis Writing* - examines the strengths and mistakes in thesis writing by discussing 19 Tantraguṇas (qualities) and 15 Tantradoṣas (flaws) sourced from Āyurvedic literature. Additionally, a comparative analysis is presented by including the list of Tantraguṇas and Tantradoṣas from Tamil literature, offering further insight into their application and relevance across different traditions.

The final chapter, *Closing Reflections and Opportunities for Advancement*, highlights how Tantrayuktis, as an indigenous thesis-writing methodology, has remained largely unknown until now. It emphasizes how its application can enable indigenous scholars to seamlessly integrate research methodologies with greater ease. The chapter also underscores the clarity and directness of Tantrayuktis' tools and proposes that Tantrayuktis-based analysis could become a new genre of research within Indian Knowledge Systems (IKS). Furthermore, the need for continued work on Tantrayuktis is discussed, focusing on the consolidation of Tantrayuktis-related knowledge across intra-linguistic, inter-linguistic, domains of IKS.

In addition to the core content, the book includes several appendices that offer further resources and tools for readers. These include links to lectures on Tantrayuktis by the author, the *Tolkāppiyam* list with definitions of *Tantiravuttis*, comparative tables of Tantrayuktis in various Saṃskṛta treatises, and a set of 50 questions for assessment. These appendices are designed to deepen the reader's engement with Tantrayuktis and facilitate the practical application of the concepts discussed in the main text.

Thus, the book attempts to present a holistic view of Tantrayuktis, providing both a theoretical framework and practical tools for integrating this ancient Indian methodology into contemporary academic research.

I owe my heartfelt gratitude to several scholars who have guided and supported me in this endeavor.

At the outset, I offer my deepest pranāms to my beloved parents Sri SS Mahadevan and Smt Vasantha, whose unwavering faith in the wisdom of Bhāratīya traditions and their enduring relevance to contemporary life led me me to pursue traditional Gurukula education. My humble pranāms to my Ācārya, Dr. Ramachandra Bhat, who taught me the Upaniṣads and other Vedantic texts during my stay and study at Veda Vijnana Gurkulam (1998-2005), and whose insightful discourses enabled me to hold the ancient Indian intellectual tradition in high esteem.

I express my sincere gratitude to Dr. S. Kalyanaraman, Director, Sarasvati Research Centre, Chennai, who initiated me into the study of of Tantrayuktis after patiently listening to my presentation on the spirit of inquiry in the Upaniṣadic dialogues around the year 2006.

I thank my research supervisor, Dr. P. Narasimhan, Retired Professor, Department of Sanskrit, University of Madras, for his invaluable guidance throughout my PhD work in the University of Madras (2005-2009).

I am deeply thankful to Prof. Shrinivasa Varkhedi Ji, Vice-Chancellor of Central Sanskrit University, New Delhi, for encouraging my work and offering me the first platform to conduct a workshop on Tantrayuktis during his tenure as the Vice-Chancellor of Kavikulaguru Kalidasa Saṃskṛta University, Nagpur. He continues his encouragement and support to this day in bringing Tantrayuktis to the centre stage in Research scenario in Saṃskṛta and IKS studies. Special thanks to eminent scholars Prof. Nagaraj Paturi Ji, INDICA and Dr Sai Susarla Ji, Siddanta Foundation and for their constant encouragement.

I am profoundly grateful to Sri Hari Kiran Vadlamani for his enthusiasm and unwavering support. His invitation through Indica Courses to conduct online programs on Tantrayuktis and his willingness to publish and promote this book have been invaluable.

A heartfelt thanks to my wife, Dr. Sowmya Krishnapur, for her steadfast scholarly support and companionship in every critical endeavor. My gratitude extends to my daughter Thrayi Jayaraman, who takes pride in even my smallest achievements. This has been a source of constant motivation.

I am also indebted to the management of SVYASA University for always encouraging my academic pursuits. My sincere thanks to Chancellor Guruji Dr. HR Nagendra Ji, Vice-Chancellor Dr. Manjunath Sharma Ji, and Registrar Prof. Shiva Sankara Sai Ji for their support and guidance.

Dr M Jayaraman
Makara Sankranti, Janary 2025

Foreword One

Pursuit of knowledge has always been one of humankind's noblest endeavors. Ṛṣis, seers, and seekers of knowledge in Bharat often regarded the seeking—jijñāsā—as the cradle of intellectual and philosophical thought. Bharat was home to such great luminaries whose works reflect this Tapasyā for knowledge. Starting from the Upaniṣads, the organization of knowledge through a methodological way gave birth to wonderful saṁvādas—dialogues. Later, structured, discipline-based knowledge emerged as śāstras.

Our Ṛṣis, such as Bhāskarācārya, Piṅgala, Kaṇāda, and many others, exemplify the meticulous and disciplined pursuit of understanding, spanning diverse domains such as mathematics, astronomy, linguistics, logic, philosophy, and more. They undeniably employed anveṣaṇavidhi—research methodologies that culminated in texts bearing witness to their remarkable intellectual achievements. Their approach to knowledge may not align with the formats embraced by the modern research community and needs some intervention in articulation and explanation. The śāstra paddhati—Shastric way of presentation—preserved the knowledge for thousands of years without any loss of information and with a scope for wider interpretation.

One method was to knit the information received from various sources in such a way that it will emerge as a new knowledge which can be faithfully transmitted to the next generation. First of all, every discipline has genesis in the core darśana, i.e., philosophy, which governs the theory part of the school. This guided theory of a school is called śāstra. Every śāstric discipline has a unique methodology of inquiry, presentation, and pedagogy.

The practical approach of a śāstra under the influence of darśana will lead to a tantra. Tantra is a śāstra in practice. This requires much more flexibility in terms of adaptability to new ideas that emerge from practice over time and the power of keeping source knowledge intact without any loss or corruption. This is much needed in the prayoga śāstras living in guru-śiṣya tradition, like nāṭya, saṅgīta, yajña, kṛṣi, vaidya-ka, etc. Even the human sciences like artha-śāstra, samāja-śāstra, nyāya-śāstra, etc., that are dynamic in nature require certain methods to keep the source knowledge intact.

The major concerns of knowledge preservation are: how to code the knowledge in sūtra or grantha form, how to transmit the same without any loss, and how to decode the same when it is needed. This methodology is called *Tantrayukti*.

Yuktis are techniques of connection. The knowledge producer and seekers should know this technique of how to connect the information to consolidate the knowledge and how to disjoin the same when needed. These *Tantrayuktis* play a very vital role in many śāstric disciplines. Many disciplines are totally dependent upon these *Tantrayuktis*. In old days, the scholars were considered to be experts in decoding and in interpretation of a śāstric work—granthi-granthi-vibhedana-chaturaḥ (ग्रन्थग्रन्थिविभेदनचतुरः). These *Tantrayuktis* are applicable to many other newly emerging knowledge systems.

By exploring and understanding the frameworks and structures inherent in them, one can understand the methodologies through which these ancient texts were constructed, which could provide a valuable input to current researchers in their quest for understanding Indian Knowledge Systems. This book explores the *Tantrayukti* techniques, the text construction methodology adopted in ancient Indian texts.

Professor Dr. M. Jayaraman (SVYASA Deemed University, Bengaluru), has done groundbreaking work in exploring *Tantrayuktis* and their relevance as a technique that can be adapted to the practical aspects of modern IKS research such as thesis writing. This book is a testimony to his painstaking efforts in this direction. I find this could be a standard Manual of thesis writing and evaluation following Indian Research Methodology, which is very much needed for IKS research.

As I read the structure of the book, I noticed its systematic arrangement that leads readers from simpler to complex concepts. Most readers may not necessarily be familiar with Sanskrit texts and keeping that in mind, the author has carefully designed the book to ensure foundational knowledge of the concept of *Tantrayukti* in the first few chapters. I recommend that readers carefully navigate through these first two chapters to understand the meaning of *Tantrayukti* and its evolution over 1500 years in the context of Sanskrit texts. The book then progresses to explain the utility and application of *Tantrayukti* techniques for easy comprehension of the concepts and content shared in the texts. The author also explains the ability to customize these techniques for their specific context. While there are many *Tantrayuktis* identified in various texts, about 32 of them have been selected for application by students in this book, making it easy for novices to navigate through the world of *Tantrayukti* and assimilate and integrate it into their thesis.

I find the book to be a practical manual with notes and observations at the end of each chapter that serve as reinforcement. Quiz and activities at the end of each chapter helps readers to test their comprehension and revisit aspects that need to be worked on. Once the ground has been prepared to equip the students with all the necessary tool, the final chapter serves as a veritable guide for the Thesis Review Process.

I congratulate Professor. M. Jayaraman for bringing out this manual and best wishes to all the scholars who wish to benefit from its content. The book could be a valuable resource for scholars who wish to pursue research in Indian Knowledge Studies. I hope, Higher Education Institutions and Researchers will welcome this new Research Manual in their reference bookshelves.

Warm regards
Prof Shrinivasa Varakhedi,
D.Litt, Vidyavachaspati
Vice Chancellor
Central Sanskrit University
New Delhi

Date: Makara Sankranti Parva, Uattarayanam, Vikrama Samvat 2081

Foreword Two

The pursuit of knowledge has been a defining feature of Indian intellectual traditions, shaping the way ideas have been structured, preserved, and transmitted across generations. From the time of the Vedic sages to the classical period of Indian śāstric literature, Indian scholars developed sophisticated methodologies for textual organization and argumentation. Among these methodologies, Tantrayukti holds a place of great significance, serving as a refined system for constructing, interpreting, and organizing knowledge systematically.

Tantrayukti, as an ancient science of text composition and analysis, is an essential intellectual tool that has underpinned some of the most profound works of Indian thought. This structured methodology has been employed across disciplines, from philosophy and logic to medicine, polity, and literary traditions. The meticulous arrangement of ideas, the logical progression of arguments, and the seamless transmission of knowledge through generations were made possible through Tantrayukti. Despite its deep roots in Indian intellectual history, the doctrine of Tantrayukti has remained an underexplored field in contemporary academia.

This book is a much-needed scholarly intervention that brings Tantrayukti back into focus, illuminating its significance not only as a historical text-construction tool but also as a methodology that can enhance contemporary research practices. The work represents a crucial step in the revival and reintegration of indigenous knowledge systems (IKS) into modern academic discourse. Prof. M. Jayaraman has undertaken the enormous task of bridging traditional Indian epistemology with contemporary research needs, offering a manual that is both theoretically rich and practically useful.

Understanding the Importance of Tantrayukti

At the heart of Tantrayukti lies the fundamental principle of structured reasoning. A systematic approach to knowledge is crucial in any scholarly endeavor, as it ensures clarity, coherence, and credibility. Ancient Indian scholars recognized that any meaningful study—whether in Nyāya (logic), Ayurveda (medicine), Arthaśāstra (political science), or Vyākaraṇa (grammar)—required well-defined methods for organizing thoughts and arguments. Tantrayukti provided the essential framework for achieving this precision.

The effectiveness of Tantrayukti is evident in how it has been seamlessly integrated into multiple fields. Kauṭilya's Arthaśāstra, one of the most sophisticated treatises on governance and economics, employs Tantrayukti techniques extensively, ensuring that every argument is logically constructed and systematically presented. Similarly, the Caraka-saṃhitā and Suśruta-saṃhitā, foundational texts of Ayurveda, apply Tantrayukti principles to organize complex medical knowledge in a coherent and accessible manner. Even in philosophical works such as Śaṅkarācārya's Brahmasūtrabhāṣya, references to Tantrayukti demonstrate its critical role in structuring arguments and counterarguments in Vedāntic exegesis.

Despite such widespread application in ancient India, Tantrayukti has largely been overlooked in modern research methodologies. Contemporary academic writing, particularly in the realm of Indian Knowledge Systems, often lacks a standardized indigenous framework for thesis construction and argumentation. This book aims to revive Tantrayukti as an essential methodology for contemporary research, offering scholars a powerful tool to enhance their academic work.

A Landmark Contribution to Research Methodology

This book is a pioneering effort in bringing the principles of Tantrayukti into mainstream academia. Prof. M. Jayaraman's work is not just an exposition of ancient textual methodologies; it is also a practical guide for researchers seeking to integrate these principles into their academic writing, particularly in thesis construction.

One of the book's most commendable features is its comprehensive approach to Tantrayukti. It not only provides an extensive analysis of historical texts but also demonstrates how these techniques can be applied in contemporary research. By systematically organizing the 32 Tantrayuktis listed in Kauṭilya's Arthaśāstra, the book provides clear definitions, practical applications, and illustrative examples from diverse disciplines. This structured approach ensures that scholars can readily apply Tantrayukti principles to their research, improving both the clarity and rigor of their work.

Furthermore, Prof. Jayaraman's deep engagement with Tamil and Pāli traditions enriches the study, revealing the pan-Indian nature of Tantrayukti. His analysis of Tandiravutti in Tamil literature, particularly in Tolkāppiyam and Nannūl, provides valuable insights into how similar methodologies were employed in Dravidian intellectual traditions. This cross-cultural approach underscores the universal applicability of Tantrayukti and its relevance across linguistic and philosophical traditions.

The Author's Dedication and Scholarly Rigor

The impact of this book is a direct result of Prof. M. Jayaraman's lifelong dedication to the study of Indian Knowledge Systems. With a deep foundation in Sanskrit, traditional śāstraic learning, and contemporary research methodologies, he has successfully navigated the complex terrain of Tantrayukti, making it accessible to modern scholars. His journey—beginning with his doctoral research on Tantrayukti in Kauṭilya's Arthaśāstra and Tamil Tolkāppiyam—has culminated in this masterful work, which synthesizes years of rigorous study, teaching, and interaction with scholars from diverse backgrounds.

His ability to present dense śāstric concepts in a clear and structured manner makes this book a valuable resource not only for students and researchers but also for educators seeking to incorporate IKS methodologies into their curriculum. Through numerous workshops, lectures, and research projects, Prof. Jayaraman has played a pivotal role in reviving Tantrayukti, ensuring that it regains its rightful place in the academic study of Indian epistemology.

A Guide for the Future of Indian Research

The integration of Tantrayukti into academic research has the potential to revolutionize Indian Knowledge Studies. By employing these time-tested methodologies, researchers can enhance the precision, coherence, and analytical depth of their work. This book not only educates scholars about the historical significance of Tantrayukti but also provides them with the tools necessary to incorporate these methodologies into contemporary research and thesis writing.

Moreover, the book aligns perfectly with the National Education Policy (NEP) 2020, which emphasizes the integration of Indian Knowledge Systems into mainstream academia. As institutions across India begin to adopt IKS methodologies, this book will serve as a foundational text for scholars looking to structure their research within an indigenous framework.

In addition to serving as an academic guide, this book is also an invitation to further research. The field of Tantrayukti studies is still in its nascent stages, and Prof. Jayaraman's work lays the groundwork for future scholars to build upon. Whether through comparative studies, cross-disciplinary applications, or pedagogical innovations, there is vast potential for expanding the application of Tantrayukti beyond its traditional domains.

Conclusion

In the modern era, where academic research is often influenced by Western methodologies, it is imperative to revive and reintegrate indigenous approaches that have long been overlooked. Tantrayukti, as a time-honored system of textual construction and logical analysis, offers a uniquely Indian approach to scholarship that is both rigorous and insightful.

This book, through its meticulous research, practical applications, and interdisciplinary insights, is a monumental contribution to the study of Indian Knowledge Systems. It is a must-read for anyone involved in academic writing, research methodology, and the study of Indian epistemology.

I congratulate Prof. M. Jayaraman for this outstanding scholarly achievement. May this book inspire a new generation of researchers to embrace Tantrayukti, ensuring that this invaluable tradition continues to thrive in the modern academic landscape.

Dr Ahalya.S
Vice Chancellor,
Karnataka Samskrit University, Bengaluru

Photos

Lecture on Tantrayukti at the Master's Training Program on *Tantrayukti and Methods of IKS,* organized by the IKS Division, Government of India, at Central Sanskrit University, Bhopal, on February 26, 2024.

Talk on the Indic Method of Thesis Construction: Tantrayukti at the *Bhāratīya Anusandhāna Paddhati* (Indian Research Methodology) seminar, held from November 15–18, 2023, at the Department of Sanskrit Studies, University of Hyderabad.

Meeting with the Hon'ble Governor of Tamil Nadu, Sri R.N. Ravi, to discuss my literary contributions, including *Tantrayukti*, on September 7, 2022.

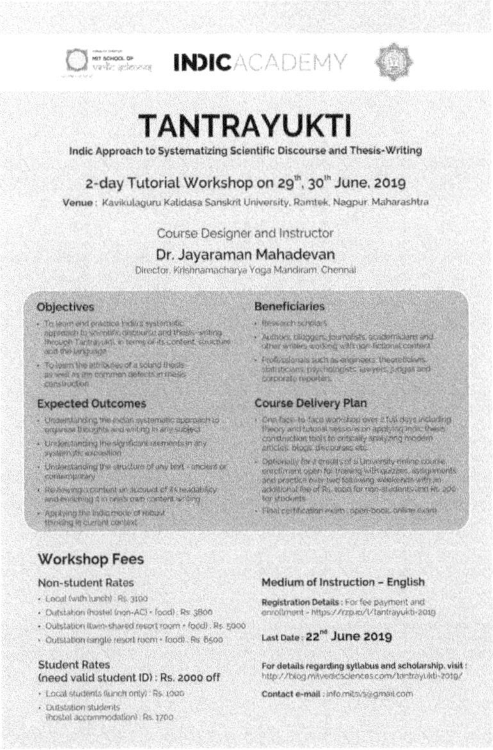

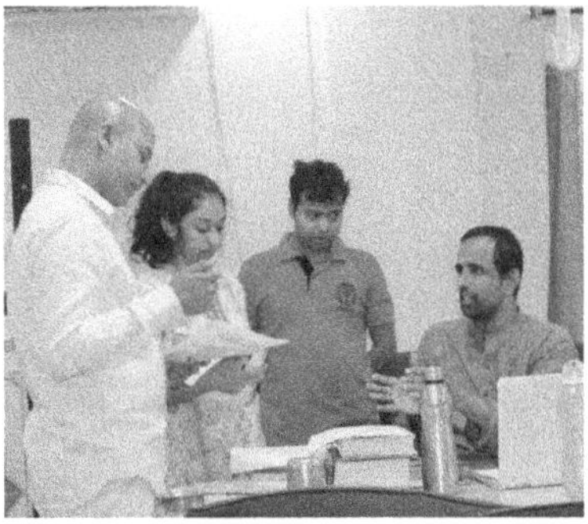

The first-ever full-fledged workshop on Tantrayukti, hosted by Kavikulaguru Kalidas Sanskrit University (KKSU) and supported by Indica Academy, held on September 29–30, 2019.

Workshop on the Elements of Research methodology in Ancient Indian Sources for PhD scholars and faculty at SVYASA Yoga University, held on September 26, 2017.

Chapter 1

Tantrayuktis: A Gateway to Traditional Textual Methodology

"Had the ancient Indians conceived a form of scientific composition? Had they developed a method of treatment of the scientific subject in an orderly manner? Did they expound all the aspects of the given subject or did they confine their discussion to a few of them only? Did they reproduce the views of the past and/or the contemporary thinkers? What was their mode of making cross references? What style did they resort to, to establish their new thoughts and theories? Did the idea of rendering the subject matter intelligible as well as enjoyable ever strike them? Had the ancient Indian intellectuals devised any methodology of writing scientific works?"

(Lele 1981:2).

Prof.Lele raised these questions having in mind the doctrine of Tantrayuktis as the answer.

Satishchandra Vidyabhushana states that "Tantrayuktis which literally signifies 'scientific arguments' was compiled possibly in the 6th century BCE. (i.e. even before *Arthaśāstra*) to systematize debates in pariṣads or learned councils."

(Vidyabhushana 1921;24)

Prof.W.K.Lele is of the opinion that since there are indications of Tantrayuktis in aṣṭādhyāyī of Pāṇini(Lele 1981:5), his era being 5th century B.C.E. Approximately the doctrine should have evolved in the post- Pāṇini era. Thus we conjecture that the form in which Tantrayuktis are found in the *Arthaśāstra* is the result of continuous rumination and evolution over centuries, the literary evidence for which is not traceable, right from the post- Pāṇinian era till the appearance of *Arthaśāstra* in the 3rd century B.C.E Gerhard Oberhammer opines that Tantrayuktis doctrine is parallel to the Vāda doctrine on the basis of which the entire Nyāya tradition stands. To quote him:

"Indians tried to analyse the formal elements which gave form to a scientific work in the same way that they tried to analyse the elements of debate; for practical usage they collected these elements in lists and explained them."

(Obberhammer 1968:600).

Vātsyāyana, the commentator of the Nyāyasūtras-s quotes Tantrayuktis (nyāyasūtra-bhāśyam 1.1.4). This establishes the fact that it is an independent doctrine developed by ancient Indians which was respected and referred to by the Nyāya tradition. This goes to show the position the doctrine of Tantrayuktis occupied in ancient Indian literature.

Definitions of Tantrayuktis

Scholars have rendered Tantrayuktis in various terms,

i. 'Plan of a treatise' (Shamashastry 1909:459)
ii. 'Forms of Scientific argument' (Vidyabhushana 1921:24)
iii. 'Formal elements which gave form to a scientific work' (Obberhammer 1968:600)
iv. 'Methodology and technique, which enable one to compose and interpret scientific treatises correctly and intelligently'. – (Muthuswamy 1974:i)
v. 'Method of treatment, maxims for the interpretation of textual topics' (Solomon 1978:73)
vi. Methodology of theoretico-scientific treatisies in Saṃskṛta (Lele 1981: Cover page)

vii. An expedient in the writing of science – (Mittal 2000:23)
viii. 'Methodology in Saṃskṛta texts on Science' (Sharma 2006:30)

The above statements would suffice to adequately introduce Tantrayuktis. The above list of definitions organized in a chronological order indicates that Saṃskṛta academia since the beginning of 20th century was aware of Tantrayuktis as a textual methodology. But seldom was it utilized as a textual methodology of traditional literature which can also provide inputs for text construction and interpretation in mainstream academia or not even in Saṃskṛta academia. It is only in recent times with the renewed interest in Indian Knowledge Systems that Tantrayuktis is looked into with seriousness as a methodology for IKS.

Etymology of Tantrayuktis

Tantrayuktis is a compound of two words in Saṃskṛta namely *Tantra* and Yukti.

Tantra

Tantra has a wide range of meanings. One definition of the term is

तनोति विपुलानर्थान् तत्त्वमन्त्रसमन्वितान्।
त्राणञ्च कुरुते यस्मात् तन्त्रमित्यभिधीयते॥[1]

(Lele 1981:19)

Tantra can be termed as that which discusses and details subjects and concepts and also that which protects.

Further –

तत्रायुर्वेदः शाखा विद्या सूत्रं ज्ञानं शास्त्रं लक्षणं तन्त्रमित्यनर्थान्तरम्[2]

(*Caraka-saṃhitā*, siddhi-sthāna 12.29-30)

1 tanoti vipulānarthān tattvamantrasamanvitān |
trāṇañca kurute yasmāt Tantramityabhidhīyate ||
2 tatrāyurvedaḥ śākhā vidyā sūtraṃ jñānaṃ śāstraṃ lakṣaṇaṃ Tantramityanarthāntaram |

Tantra is synonymously used with Āyurveda, *a branch of Veda, education, aphorism, knowledge,* śāstra *and definition.*

But there are certian other viewpoints in presenting the meaning of the term *Tantra* in the compound Tantrayuktis. Some authors restrict the meaning of the term *Tantra* only to Āyurveda.

Aruṇadatta, the author of sarvāṅgasundarī, feels, *Tantra* as, that by which the body is protected i.e. Āyurveda –

tantryate dhāryate śarīramaneneti *Tantram* ā*yurvedaḥ*

(Āyurvedadīpikā, *siddhisthānam* 12.40)

Another derivation has been provided to the same end

Tantrī kuṭumbadhāraṇe tasmin Tantramiti rūpam ।
kuṭumbaṃ śarīram । *taddhārayati hitopadeśāhitanivāraṇadvārā* ।

(Muthuswamy 1974:i)

This alternative, bases its derivation on one of the roots from which the words *Tantra* is derived i.e. *Tantrī kuṭumbadhāraṇe*. That which protects the body (*kuṭumba*) by the way of advising what is good and warding away what is not desirable is *Tantra*. This derivation also invariably points to the meaning Āyurveda.

But scholars who have commented upon Tantrayuktis feel that it is not proper to limit the meaning of the term *Tantra* only to Āyurveda. Muthuswamy opines that such delimitation of the meaning is done by some commentators who –

"Interpret the term in a roundabout way to bring āyurveda alone in its fold".

(Muthuswami1974: iii)

This is in spite of his admission of the long-standing association Tantrayuktis with Āyurveda texts. This is clear from the following statement

"The unique style and technique of exposition which developed in Āyurveda, as in other branches of study, ...are called āyurveda Tantrayuktis... Tantrayuktis is as ancient as the literature of āyurveda itself."

(Muthuswami1974: iii)

The reason adduced by him to support the view that *Tantra* denotes any śāstraic text is that, in the texts like Amarakośa, Medinīkośa and texts authored by Vāgbhaṭa the term *Tantra* is used to denote simply a science and not Āyurveda alone. Further he is of the opinion that other texts like *Arthaśāstra* of *Kauṭilya*, which is a text on polity, have made use of Tantrayuktis. Thus though etymologically the definition can be derived in such a way as to denote Āyurveda, from the point of view of its application it is beyond doubt that *Tantra* denotes any branch of science. Thus etymological and conventional usages point to the fact that *Tantra* is used to denote a systematic work of literature.

Yuktis

Yukti, in the context of Tantrayuktis is defined as follows -

युज्यन्ते सङ्कल्प्यन्ते संबध्यन्ते परस्परमर्थाः
सम्यक्तया प्राकरणिकेऽभिमतेऽर्थे
विरोधव्याघातादिदोषजातमपास्यअनयेति युक्तिः।[3]

"... that which removes blemishes like impropriety, contradiction, etc., from the intended meaning and thoroughly joins the meanings together.".

(Sharma 1949:1)

Thus the compound *Tantrayuktis* denotes those devices that aid the composition of a text in a systematic manner to convey intended ideas clearly.

3 yujyante saṅkalpyante saṃbadhyante parasparamarthā:
samyaktayā prākaraṇike'bhimate'rthe virodhavyāghātādidoṣajātamapāsyaanayeti Yukti: |

Tantrayuktis List

Tantrayuktis are given as a list in ancient texts. Some texts define and illustrate their usage in the text while others merely produce the list. The oldest available Tantrayuktis list (32 devices) of *Arthaśāstra* is as follows -

Adhikaraṇa (Topic), *vidhānam* (statement of contents), *yogaḥ* (employment of sentences), *padārthaḥ* (meaning of the word), *hetvarthaḥ* (reason), *uddeśaḥ* (mention), *nirdeśaḥ* (explanation), *upadeśaḥ* (advice), *apadeśaḥ* (reference), *atideśaḥ* (application), *pradeśaḥ* (indication), *upamānam* (analogy), *arthāpattiḥ* (implication), *saṃśayaḥ* (doubt), *prasaṅgaḥ* (situation), *viparyayaḥ* (contrary), *vākyaśeṣaḥ* (completion of a sentence), *anumatam* (agreement), *vyakhyānam* (emphasis), *nirvacanam* (derivation), *nidarśanam* (illustration), *apavargaḥ* (exception), *svasaṃjñā* (technical term), *pūrvapakṣaḥ* (prima facie view), *uttarapakṣaḥ* (correct view), *ekāntaḥ* (invariable rule), *anāgatāvekṣaṇam* (reference to a future statement), *atikrantāvekṣaṇam* (reference to a past statement), *niyogaḥ* (restriction), *vikalpaḥ* (option), *samuccayaḥ* (combination), ūhyam (determinable fact)

(Arthaśāstra Adhikaraṇa 15)

As can be seen, the above list contains 32 devices. In the text, the list is followed by a discussion on the doctrine of Tantrayuktis. The author of the *Arthaśāstra* enumerates Tantrayuktis, provides the definitions and shows the place of application of those Yuktis in his treatise. This is the earliest and yet complete treatment of Tantrayuktis. Scholars feel that though *Arthaśāstra* is the earliest reference regarding Tantrayuktis it cannot be deemed as the text that originated the doctrine.

Components of Tantrayuktis

Tantrayuktis doctrine consists of three basic elements viz.,

a. Tantrayuktis- Tantrayuktis are the tools that help an author present his ideas in the form of a systematic text.

b. *Tantraguṇa* - Tantraguṇas are the characteristics of a good treatise.
c. Tantradoṣa- Tantradoṣa-s are the flaws that impair a systematic treatise.

Initially, Tantrayuktis were the whole and sole of the doctrine. Later, scholars added Tantraguṇas and Tantradoṣas to the doctrine to widen its scope of applicability.

INSIGHTS

Text construction Tools in IKS beyond Tantrayuktis

Did you know that other than Tantrayuktis there were many other hints on text construction? Explore these themes -

a) **Three teir- text construction** - **Sūtra**– a text in the form of brief tight statements, **Vārttika** – Gloss that revises the errors that might have crept in sūtra text, **Bhāṣya** - commentary that consolidates and elaborates the wisdom of Sūtra and Vārttika (References: Sūtra, Vārttika: Sarvalakṣaṇasangraha, p.115,.97, Bhāṣya: Nyāyakōśa, p.306)

b) **Construct a segment of a text or Adhikaraṇa** – that includes 5 aspects - *Viṣaya* - subject matter of the topic, *Viśaya* is the list of different opinions on the subject matter, *Pūrvapakṣa and Uttara*: Pūrvapakṣa refers to the set of systematic expositions supporting all the opinions except the one finally desired to be established, Uttara refers to is the systematic refutation of all the "opponent's views". *Prayojana* clarifies what material difference it makes if an opinion is embraced. *Saṅgati* is a mention of how the current sub-topic is relevant to the current topic of discussion (Reference: Sarvalakṣaṇasangraha, p.7)

c) **To systematically present answers to questions** – *Uttara-lakṣaṇa-* Answers shall be given after analysing all the facets of the question, it must be comprehensive. No element of doubt shall exist in the mind of the student after hearing the answer. It must not require any further explanation. (Reference Vācaspatyam, Volume 2, p.1062)

Chapter 2

Tantrayuktis through Ages

Shaping Methodologies for Knowledge Construction

While it is important to know Tantrayuktis as a textual methodology, the history of utilization and the ways of its utilization in the literature of the past is to be looked into. Such an activity has twofold utility. They are as follows -

a. This will indicate that Tantrayuktis was not mere intellectual conception. It was also applied in diverse literature as a methodology
b. The diverse ways in which it was utilized will also give us ideas for utilizing Tantrayuktis is various ways.

The study of utilization of Tantrayuktis will also show that it impact was was not limited to Saṃskṛta texts, it also extended to other literary traditions including Tamil and Pāli.

In Saṃskṛta Literature – 1500 years

Tantrayuktis was compiled possibly as early as in the 6th century B.C.E (Vidyābhūṣaṇa 1921;24). Texts belonging to various periods and disciplines have made use of these Yukti. A chronological presentation is attempted below:

(i) *Arthaśāstra*

It is *Arthaśāstra* that first gave a full-fledged treatment of Tantrayuktis. It is a known fact that *Arthaśāstra* is an ancient Indian work on polity and statecraft. The last *adhikaraṇa* of *Kauṭilya Arthaśāstra* has been styled Tantrayuktis, which defines and illustrates thirty-two Tantrayuktis. There are divergent views about the date of *Arthaśāstra,*. the pendulum swinging between fifth century B.C.E and seventh century C.E. Some scholars say that the text was composed during the reign of Candragupta Maurya, i.e., between 321 B.C.E and 296 B.C.E (Lele 1981:8-9). But generally 5th century BCE is accepted as the period of composition of the text.

(ii) *Nyāyasūtrabhāśya*

Vātsyāyana, the commentator of *Nyāyasūtra*, is also familiar with Tantrayuktis. He quotes a Tantrayuktis namely *anumata* while discussing the fourth sūtra of the first āhnika in the first chapter of *Gautama's* Nyāyasūtra. The date of *Nyāyasūtrabhāśya* is generally accepted to be 4th century B.C.E

(iii) *Caraka-saṃhitā*

Caraka-saṃhitā comes next in the order of chronology. In the verses 41 – 45 of the twelfth chapter of the siddhisthāna, thirty-six Tantrayuktis are enumerated. The sequence of enumeration of Tantrayuktis in *Caraka-saṃhitā* differs from that of *Arthaśāstra.* Nomenclatures of some of the Yuktis are also not similar. *Caraka* flourished around First Century B.C.E

(iv) *Suśrutasaṃhitā*

Suśrutasaṃhitā is a renowned work on ancient Indian surgery. It has been written in the form of questions and answers between Dhanvantari *and* Suśruta. The period of composition of Suśrutasaṃhitā is 4th century C.E. The author has in the sixty-fifth chapter listed thirty-two Tantrayuktis. Though the number of Yuktis is same as that of *Arthaśāstra*, the order of enumeration is different.

(v) *Aṣṭāṅgasaṅgraha*

It is a text on Āyurveda written by Vāgbhaṭa. In the 50th chapter of the *Uttarasthāna* of this work are mentioned thirty-six Tantrayuktis. *Vāgbhaṭa* is said have existed in the period between 3rd and 4th century CE. *Aṣṭāṅgahṛdaya*, another work by the same author, also mentions Tantrayuktis.

(vi) *Viṣṇudharmottarapurāṇa*

In this purāṇa among so many topics, thirty-two Tantrayuktis are also defined but not illustrated. These Tantrayuktis appear in the sixth chapter of the third khaṇda. The work is dated between 4th and 5th century C.E.

(vii) *Yuktidīpikā*

It is a rare commentary on *Sāṅkhyakārikā* of Īśvarakṛṣṇa. It is approximately dated around 6th century C.E. Ram Chandra Pandya (Pandya 1967:3), who has critically edited this text, tentatively names one 'Rājā'as the author of the work. In the introduction to the text, the author mentions twelve devices and names them variously as *Tantrasampat*, *Tantraguṇa and* Tantrayuktis.

(viii) *Brahmasūtrabhāṣya Ācārya Śaṅkara*

Ācārya Śaṅkara (500 BCE/7-8 CE) foremost among the Philosophers of Bharat was aware of Tantrayuktis and has utilized a Tantrayuktis in his work Brahmasūtrabhāṣya. In his commentary to the Sūtra पञ्चवृत्तिर्मनोवद्व्यपदिश्यते[4] (2.4.12) he utilizes Tantrayuktis Anumata. The lines from the commentary in this regard is as follows – 'परमतमप्रतिषिद्धमनुमतं भवति' इति न्यायात्[5]. It is to be noted that the wordings of the definition of the Anumata is the same as that of the definition of Kauṭilya.

---

4 pañcavṛttirmanovadvyapadiśyate

5 'paramatamapratiṣiddhamanumataṃ bhavati' iti nyāyāt

(ix) *Tantrayuktisvicāra*

It is an independent text on Tantrayuktis. It was written by *Nīlamegha Bhiṣak*. His definitions and illustrations follow the *Caraka-saṃhitā*. He has enlisted thirty-six Tantrayuktis in his treatise. He composed his work during 9th century C.E.

There is another independent text called Tantrayuktis*ḥ*. The author of the text is unknown. So is the exact date of the work. This text also defines Tantrayuktis and it belongs to Āyurveda tradition. In many places the definitions of this text differ from the previous one.

(x) *Īśvarapratyabhijñāvivṛtivimarśinī, Svacchandatantra and Vamakeśvarimata-vivaraṇa*

These are the three texts of *Tantra*śāstra that have made use of Tantrayuktis.

Īśvarapratyabhijñāvivṛtivimarśinī is a text on Kashmir śaivism. *Abhinavagupta* wrote the text. *Utpaladeva* wrote a text *iśvarapratyabhijñā* to preach Śaiva *Siddhānta*. The text comprises of 190 couplets. The same author supplied the gloss and commentary to the text. *Abhinavagupta* first explained the couplets. The text was called Īśvarapratyabhijñāvimarśinī. Later he explained the gloss and commentary too, which is the present text. This text cites two instances where Tantrayuktis *Anāgatāvekṣaṇa* is cited (Shastri 1942:147).

Svacchandatantra or the *Tantra* of the autonomous is a text on Śaivasiddhānta. It is in the form of a dialogue between *Svacchandabhairava* (Śiva) and *Bhairavī (*Śakti*)*. It is mainly concerned with rituals of initiation and the desiderative practices of a *Sādhaka*. *Rājanaka kṣemarāja* (1000-1050 C.E) a disciple of *Abhinavagupta*, has written a commentary on the text. The commentary is to prove that this school of practice is non-dualistic. In three instances we find the utilization of Tantrayuktis in this text. (Svacchandatantra 1.52, 1.65, 2.130)

Vamakeśvara-tantra is one among the most frequently cited and commented upon sources in contemporary South Indian Śrīvidyā tradition (Śāktatantra). It is also one among the most important text on the Śrīkula tradition of Śrīvidyopāsanā. It is considered the oldest Saṃskṛta source text in the tradition. *Jayaratha*, the 12th century Kasmiri scholar, best known as the author of the *Vivaraṇa* of *Abhinavagupta*'s *Tantrāloka*. He calls the source text (*Vamakeśvara-tantra*) as *Vamakeśvaramata*. Accordingly, he has styled his commentary as *Vamakeśvarimata-vivaraṇa* (commentary on the *Vamakeśvaramata*). While commenting upon the 58th verse of the first Paṭala and 37th verse of the 4th Paṭala, Jayaratha uitilizes Tantrayuktis - Anāgatāvekṣaṇa.

Thus right from 5th century B.C.E to 12th century C.E. century (i.e. for 1700 years) we find references of Tantrayuktis. A doctrine that was in vogue for such a long period of time fell into disuse and was consequently forgotten.

Elements of Tantrayuktis in Other Texts

So far, various texts that have made direct reference to Tantrayuktis were discussed. Below are few texts in which indications to the presence andapplication of Tantrayuktis can be percieved. These texts also belong to various braches including Grammar, poetics etc.

Pāṇini and Tantrayuktis

Aṣṭādhyāyi (a treatise in eight chapters) is a work on Saṃskṛta grammar, which is known and respected all over the world. Pāṇini (fifth century B.C.E) the author of Aṣṭādhyāyi, is considered an original thinker. He was held in high esteem by Patañjali (Mahaṭa Yatnena Sūṭram Praṇayati Sma - Mahābhaṣya 1.1.1)'. This observation suggests that Pāṇini had composed each Sūtra only after careful consideration. This work, therefore, exhibits exemplarary discipline of a scientific compostion. Agrawala (1953)[6] states that Pāṇini knew more than a dozen devices that

6 Agrawala, V. S. (1953). India as known to Pāṇini (pp. 308–310). University of Lucknow.

went into planning and structing a treatise - viz. Adhikāraṇa, Vidhāna, Hetvārtha, Upadeśa, Apadeśa, Saṃśaya, Vākyādhyāhāra, Anumatā, Atiśayavarṇana (Vyākhyā), Nirvacana, svasaṃjñā, Pūrvapakṣa, Uttarapakṣa, Atideśa and Vikalpa.

With the present state of knowledge, it can be assumed that in the formation of the doctrine of Tantrayuktis the treatise of Pāṇini might have played an invisible role by way of influencing the thinking process of formulators of the doctrine. It shall also be noticed that Gerhard Oberhammer[7] had pointed out that the works of grammar in the Pāṇini tradition influenced the Yuktis of Yuktidīpikā.

Kāmasūtras and Tantrayuktis

Kāmasūtras like Kauṭilya Arthaśāstra is a text on social science. It has 1250 verses, distributed in 36 chapters, which are further organized into 7 sections. Vātsyāyana composed it around second century C.E. Though there are no direct references to Tantrayuktis doctrine, Prof. Lele[8], on the basis of his structural analysis of the treatise, observes that in more than 200 occasions the thirty-six devices mentioned in the doctrine of Tantrayuktis have been utilized through out the text by the author. Further, he opines that Vātsyāyana introduces another new Yuktis in his treatise called Prāyovāda. Thus, not only have Tantrayuktis been utilized but Kāmasūtras has also added newer aspects to the doctrine.

Texts on Poetics and Tantrayuktis

Prof. Lele'[9]in his analysis of the Tantrayuktis cites numerous examples from the works on poetics to illustrate various devices. He is of the opinion that the field of poetics provides ample oppurtunity to understand the nature of problems related to Tantrayuktis. In his conlcusion to the

7 Oberhammer, G. (1967–1968). Notes on Tantrayukti-s. The Adyar Library Bulletin, 31–32, 600. (Dr. Raghavan Felicitation Volume).

8 Lele, W. K. (2006). Methodology of Ancient Indian Sciences (pp. 159–164). Varanasi: Chaukhamba Surabharati Prakashana.

9 Ibid p.214

analysis of the Tantrayuktis he identifies certain areas in which the doctrine could be of vital help. Six of the eight suggestions that he gives are related to the field of poetics. They include

a. A Tantrayuktis oriented interpretation of Vāmana 's Kāvyālaṁkārasūtra.
b. Theories and contraversies in Indian poetics.
c. The untold Saṃskṛta peotics
d. The optional and obligatory rules of Indian poetics
e. A critical study of the prominent works of Indian poetics.

The study of various texts on poetics on the basis of the Tantrayuktis doctrine has led him to the above conclusions. In the process of study, he culls instances from treatises on poetics small and vast in volume like a) Dhvanyāloka of **Ānandavardhana** b) Kāvyālaṁkāra of Bhāmaha c) Kāvyānuśāsana of Hemacandra d) Vakrōktijivita of Kuntaka e) Kāvyālaṁkāra of Rudraṭa f) Kāvyamimāmsā of Rājaśēkhara g) Alankararatnākara of Śobhākramitra h) Kāvyālaṁkārasūtra of Vāmana and i) **Sāhityadarpaṇa** of Viśvanatha are a few texts that he quotes to illustrate Tantrayuktis. This is proof enough to show the extent to which the branch of poetics has taken recourse to the doctrine of Tantrayuktis.

In Tamil Literature - 1900 years

As has been stated in the introduction the application of Tantrayuktis-doctrine was not limited only to Saṃskṛta treatises. Ancient Tamil literary tradition also utilized it to a great extent. *Tantiravuttis or Uttis* were part of methods or conventions of presentation and interpretations of literary topics in Tamil literature. Such conventions, in general, were called *Nūnmarapu.* These conventions were assiduously adhered to while composing texts. All the major authors of grammar texts in Tamil literature stated these canons. The *Nūnmarapu* normally appeared in the beginning of the work. Some texts mention it at the end also. The other elements of the *Nūnmarapu* includes the ten types of beauties, ten types of errors, types of texts, seven types of opinions etc. Tantrayuktis has been an integral part of *Nūnmarapu* from the earliest periods.

Generally, the term *Utti* is considered as a word borrowed from Saṃskṛta Yuktis (*Vaṭamozhicitaivu*). But some Scholars have attempted to define the term from Tamil root. Śivaliṅganār (Note: translation of the Tamil quote has been given below) says

*"that the term Utti is derived from the Tamil root 'uy' to apply or to think. That which becomes applied becomes Uytti (uykkappaṭuvatu uyttiyāyiṟṟu) (*Bhagavati 1981:180).

Various scholars in their expositions have defined these *Utti*-s. T.V. Gopala Iyer presents the following definition –

nūṟcaitikaḻaic cevvvamai collutal Utti
(Presenting the intended concepts of a text
clearly/systematically is Utti).

(Gopaliyyer 2005:228)

Tamil texts

Tamil literature also has a long history of utilization of the *Tantiravuttis* similar to that of the Saṃskṛta tradition. Based on current knowledge, it extended from 1st century CE to 18th or 19th century CE. Though the reference in Tamil texts on Tantrayuktis begin later when compared to *Arthaśātra*, it extends well beyond its utilization in the Saṃskṛta texts references to which dry up around the 12th century in Saṃskṛta literature. Let us briefly consider the works that have been known to have utilized the *Tantiravuttis*.

(i) *Tolkāppiyam,* the oldest available Tamil work, deals with Tantrayuktis in the *Maraṟpiyal* chapter of *Porulatikāram* in *Sūtra* number 665. *Tolkāppianar* also enlists 32 *Uttikaḷ (*Yuktis*)*, a la *Arthaśāstra* of *Kauṭilya*. But V.R. Ramachandra Dikshtar (Dikshtar 1930:82) opines that only 22 *Uttikaḷ* of *Tolkāppiyam* match with that of *Arthaśāstra*. The date of *Tolkāppiam* is considered as 1st century C.E.

(ii) *Nannūl* is another grammar text, which is second only to *Tolkāppiyam* in the order of prominence in *Tamil* literature. This work is ascribed to *Sage Pavananti.* This text too mentions 32 Tantrayuktis. The order of enumeration and treatment of *Tantiravuttis* differ from that of *Tolkāppiyam.* The date of Nannūl has been fixed at 6th century C.E.

There are other texts in Tamil tradition that mention or make use of Tantrayuktis are as follows, (iii) *Yapperungalakkārigai* (11th century C.E), (iv) *Māranalaṅkāram* (1540-65 C.E), (v) *Ilakkaṇaviḻakkam* (17th century) and (vi) *Cuvaminātham* (18th or 19th Century CE). The above are a few known texts that have utilized the doctrine of *Tantiravuttis.* [10] The Yuktis of Tolkāppiyam and Kauṭilya Arthaśāstra was compared and alazyed by the author of the book in his PhD thesis.[11] Based on the analysis of the definitions of the respective Yuktis it was found that 20 Yuktis of both the texts match.[12]

Pāli Literature

Most texts in Pāli literature are about Buddha's teachings or Buddhist cannons. The Tripiṭaka are the major texts in this tradition. Apart from this, various schools of thought branched out from the Buddhist tradtion, which had thier own cannonical works along with the three major texts. For the interpretation of these texts by later authors, methodology was thought out which was penned down in the form of the above two texts. Scholars are of the view that these methodological texts were influenced by the Tantrayuktis doctrine. It is evident from the follwing words of B.C.Law'[13] -

The Nettipakarana is essentially a Pāli treatise on the textual and excegetical methodology, a Buddhist treatment upon the whole of Tantrayuktis discussed in the Kauṭilya Arthaśāstra, the Suśrutasaṃhitā, the Caraka-saṃhitā, and the Aṣṭāngahṛdaya.

---

10 A detailed list and definition of Tantrayuktis of Tamil literature can be seen in Appendix

11 Jayaraman, M. (2009) The Doctrine of Tantrayukti – A Study. Ph.D. Thesis Submitted to the University of Madras.

12 The table of the matching Yuktis is given in the Appendix

13 A history of Pali literature, B.C. Law, Indica, Varanasi, 2000, chapter iv, pg.352

Further the statement of A.K.Warder also brings to light the similarity between the the two streams of texual methodology

"It (Peṭakopadeśa) should be compared with paralell developments in the same period in the Brahmanical tradtion of Vedic exegesies and of the organisation of knowledge generally: Mimāmsā (investigation, exegesis) with its elaboration of the rules of interpretation of Vedic texts; Tantrayuktis *(combination-scheme-congruence-*Yukti *of the system -Tantra), the methodology of constructing a branch of science or a treatise on it, the earliest discussion on which, now extant, appearing to be the appendix to Kauṭilya 's Arthaśāstra."*[14]

14 Indian buddhism, A.K. Warder, Motilal Banarsidas, New Delhi, 1991, p.316

INSIGHTS

Tantrayuktis for Āyurveda and Beyond !

Esther Solomon states that *"The fact that the expostion is given of Tantrayuktis in works on medicine and politics besides those on logic is sufficient evidence, to show that it was concerned with the interpretation of textual topics and with the methods of debating as applicable to all sciences."*

(Reference: Indian Dialectics, p.73)

Gerhard Oberhammer another scholar who has analysed Tantrayuktis, also provides clear indication of the fact that Tantrayuktis was common to all sciences. He states that *"Tantrayuktis, again similar to the Vāda doctrines, had their influences on later times, without which the written, scientific style of the classical period in India would be hard to understand"*.

(Reference: Notes on Tantrayuktis, p.603)

Chapter 3

Functional Dynamics of Tantrayuktis

Functions of Tantrayuktis as has been discussed in the texts and secondary sources are presented in this chapter. This will help to understand the purpose that Saṃskṛta tradition intended it to be utilized.

Prabodha and Prakāśa

The following verse from *Caraka-saṁhitā* succinctly presents the role of Tantrayuktis -

यथाम्बुजवनस्यार्कः प्रदीपो वेश्मनो यथा।
प्रबोधप्रकाशार्थाः तथा तन्त्रस्य युक्तयः॥[15]

(Caraka-saṁhitā Siddhisthāna 12. 46)

Just as the sun causes the bed of lotuses to bloom or just as the lamp lights up a house, so also Tantrayuktis shed light on the meanings of the texts.

To the above quoted verse from the *Caraka-saṁhitā*, *Cakrapāṇidatta*, the author of a commentary on *Caraka-saṁhitā* called Āyurvedadīpikā makes certain insightful observations. They are as follows -

1. *"yathāmbujavanasyārkaḥ"*(Just as the sun causes the bed of lotuses to bloom).To this example *Cakrapāṇidatta* adds the following comment.

15 yathāmbujavanasyārkaḥ pradīpo veśmano yathā |
prabodhaprakāśārthāḥ tathā Tantrasya yuktayaḥ ||

yathāmbujavanasya saṅkucitasya vistārako'rkastathā tantre saṅkucitārthapradeśasya vistārakāsTantrayuktayaḥ, prabodhanāt vistārakā bhavanti ityarkadṛṣṭāntena darśayati

As the sun causes the closed petals of the bed of lotuses to spread and bloom, so does Tantrayuktis elucidate and dilate those sections of the śāstra *which seem to be cryptic.*

*(*Āyurvedadīpikā *Siddhisthāna 12. 46)*

2. "pradīpo veśmano yathā"(just as the lamp lights up a house) is the second example. To this *Cakrapāṇidatta* in his work Āyurvedadīpikā states that -

dīpadṛṣṭāntena tu, yathā dīpaḥ santameva tamasā pihitaṃ prakāśayati tathā hetvarthādikāsTantrayuktayaḥ santamarthaṃ gūḍhaṃ prakāśayantīti darśayati

From the example of the lamp it can be surmised that as the lamp brings to light an object that is very much present but enveloped by darkeness, so does Tantrayuktis act to bring out the present but unmanifest meanings in the statements of the treatise.

*(*Āyurvedadīpikā *Siddhisthāna 12. 46)*

The functions of the Tantrayuktis envisaged by Caraka as could be understood from the above verses and scholarly comments of *Cakrapāṇidatta* are as follows

a. Tantrayuktis dilate the meanings of the scientific texts, provides newer unmanifest meanings.
b. TamtraYukti doctrine is a set of universal codes for construction of any scientific treatise.
c. Tantrayuktis, the structural elements of scientific treatises, assist proper comprehension of the scientific concepts.

It "IS" meant to be a methodology document!

Two more quotations from Caraka-saṃhitā (Siddhisthana verses 47,48) is worth to be noted with regard to the functions of Tantrayuktis. Caraka states

एकस्मिन्नपि यस्येह शास्त्रे लब्धास्पदा मतिः।
स शास्त्रामन्यदप्याशु युक्तिज्ञत्वात्प्रबुध्यते।४७।[16]

If one text/discipline is studied with Tantrayuktis, then he can quickly grasp other shastras as he is aware of the systems of Yuktis

अधीयानोऽपि शास्त्राणि तन्त्रयुक्तया विना भिषक्।
नाधिगच्छति शास्त्रार्थानर्थान् भाग्यक्षये यथा।४८।[17]

Without the knowledge of Tantrayuktis even if one studies texts, he will not gain the essence like a person bereft of luck not attaining wealth.

Thus it could be understood that Tantrayuktis is meant to be a methodology document to facilitate access to the thought process of the work that is being studied.

Customizeable

Another significant observation by Caraka regarding the utilization of Tantrayuktis show the flexible and adaptable nature of the doctrine.

तन्त्रे समासव्यासोक्ते भवन्त्येता हि कृत्स्नशः
एकदेशेन दृश्यन्ते समासाभिहिते तथा।।'[18]

(*Caraka-saṁhitā Siddhisthāna* 12.45)

---

16 ekasminnapi yasyeha śāstre labdhāspadā matiḥ|47|
sa śāstramanyadapyāśu yuktijñatvāt prabudhyate|

17 adhīyāno'pi śāstrāṇi tantrayuktyā vinā bhiṣak|
nādhigacchati śāstrārthānarthān …||48||

18 tantre samāsavyāsokte bhavantyetā hi kṛtsnaśaḥ |
ekadeśena dṛśyante samāsābhihite tathā ||

"All these (Tantrayuktis) occur in a systematic work in brief and in detail. But only some of them occur in a work written in brief."

The following note on the above verse may be noted -

"It is not as if every item in the above list (of Tantrayuktis*) should have to be applied in the case of every work, nor in the same sequence. It only means that these are the methods of presentation of ideas in a work and shall have to be made use of appropriately as required in a context."*

(Sharma 2006: 31-32)

Functions of Tantrayuktis – Suśruta-samhitā

The sixty-fifth chapter of the Uttaratantra or Uttarasthāna of Suśrutasamita deals with Tantrayuktis. Suśruta discusses the purpose and functions of Tantrayuktis after giving his list of Tantrayuuktis in the same section. He discusses it in the form of question and answers

अत्रासां तन्त्रयुक्तीनां किं प्रयोजनम् ?
उच्यते वाक्ययोजनमर्थयोजनञ्च।।[19]

What is the purpose of these Tantrayuktis?
Connecting the sentences and connecting the meanings

The purpose of the doctrine is discussed at the very outset. Two-fold purpose of the doctrine is put forth. The two purposes are a) Vākyayojana (arrangement of sentences) and b) Arthayojana (organisation of meanings i.e. syntax and semantics). Ḍalhaṇa[20] commenting upon the above verse of Suśruta-samhitā elucidates the above two functions mentioned by Suśruta.

---

19 atrāsāṃ tantrayuktīnāṃ kiṃ prayojanam ?
ucyate vākyayojanamarthayojanāñca..

20 Tantrayuktivic¡ra, Appendix p. XXXI

According to him Vākyayojana means

‘वाक्यस्य असंबद्धस्य योजनं संबन्धनम्।’[21]

the joining or linking of sentences that seem to have lost the connection with previous statements or linking statements that seem to be out of context.

Arthayojana is defined by Ḍalhaṇa as

‘लीनस्यासङ्गतस्य चार्थस्य प्रकाशनं सङ्गतीकरणम्’[22]

Bringing to light the unmanifest meanings and linking those with the context.

Thus, at the very outset the two fold purpose of the text is described. Dalhaṇa assigns the Yuktis for the above two functions. Yuktis such as Yoga, Uddēśa and Nirdēśa perform the function of Vākyayojana whereas some other Yuktis such as Adhikaraṇa, Padārtha and Ūhya perform the function of Arthayojana.

Suśruta quotes (from traditional sources known to him) two more verses to further explain the function of the Tantrayuktis. The first among them is

असद्वादिप्रयुक्तानां वाक्यानां प्रतिषेधनम्।
स्ववाक्यसिद्धिरपि च क्रियते तन्त्रयुक्तितः।[23]

Refuting the views of the opponent whose views are inappropriate and establishment of one's own view is also achived by Tantrayuktis

---

21 ‘vākyasya asaṃbaddhasya yojanaṃ saṃbandhanam.’

22 ‘līnasyāsaṅgatasya cārthasya prakāśanaṃ saṅgatīkaraṇam’

23 asadvādiprayuktānāṃ vākyānāṃ pratiṣedhanam.
svavākyasiddhirapi ca kriyate tantrayuktitaḥ.

The Second verse is as follows –

व्यक्ता नोक्तास्तु येह्यर्थाः लीना ये चाप्यनिर्मलाः।
लेशोक्ता ये च केचित्स्युस्तेषाञ्चापि प्रसाधनाम्।[24]

Tantrayuktis establish clearly those ideas that are not explicitly stated, those ideas that are hidden, those ideas that are not clean (logically) or partially discussed,

In fine, it emerges that Suśruta has given five functions of Tantrayuktis namely-

1. Vākyayojana – connecting the sentence
2. Arthayojanā – connecting concepts
3. Asadvādipratiṣedha – refuting the wrong view
4. Svavākyasiddhi – establishing one's view
5. avyakta-līna-anirmala-prasādhana – unclear, hidden, incorrect ideas are rectified

Views of scholars on Fuctions of Tantrayuktis

Various functions of Tantrayuktis according to Esther Solomon are

a. Interpretation of ideas
b. Interpreting arrangement of textual words and connections
c. Description of specific peculiarities of style.

(Solomon 1978:73)

According to N.E. Muthuswami, Tantrayuktis

i. is a method of treatment of scientific subjects
ii. also, guarentees the holistic presentation of various aspects of a scientific text construction.
iii. is a tool to fine-tune the diction and style of scientific works.

(Muthuswami 1976:i)

---

24 vyaktā noktāstu yehyarthāḥ līnā ye cāpyanirmalāḥ.
leśoktā ye ca kecitsyusteṣāñcāpi prasādhanām.

On a general perusal of the doctrine it can be understood that the doctrine helps in shaping any given text in the following ways. Among the other functions, Tantrayuktis assist -

- In presenting the **content of a text**– in terms of *stating theories and rules* (Eg: niyoga, apavarga, vikalpa, upadeśa, svasaṁjṣā) and explaining/substantiating/justifying those theories (Eg: nirvacana, pūrvapakṣa, anumata, uttarapakṣa, dr̥ṣṭānta)
- In defining the **basic structure** of a work (Eg: adhikaraṇa, vidhāna, uddeśa, nirdeśa)
- In fine-tuning **diction and style of expression** in a treatise (Eg: vākyaśeṣa, arthāpatti, samuccaya, atikrāntāvekṣaṇa, anāgatāvekṣaṇa)

Thus it could be seen that Tantrayuktis-doctrine touches upon all fundamental aspects required for a systematic and compact treatise. Let us discuss these with appropriate illustrations in the next chapter.

Chapter 4

Devices of Tantrayuktis

Illustrations, Explanations & Implications

This chapter directly introduces Tantrayuktis by classifying them based on the three major divisions presented as the functions of Tantrayuktis document - Viz

- For arriving at the content of a thesis
- For structuring the thesis
- For fine-tuning the language and refining the diction

As mentioned earlier, there are so many ancient sources for the devices of Tantrayuktis (in varying in number) that provides the list of devices, defines and illustrates the Yuktis with examples. For sake of simplicity of approach, clarity, uniformity and keeping in mind the document should be readily usable for research purposes - the Yuktis are presented, defined and illustrated based on the following criterion –

- The list of the Yuktis are presented from the oldest available Saṃskṛta source of Tantrayuktis - the Arthaśāstra[25]
- The definitions provided to the Yuktis are also based Arthaśāstra unless otherwise mentioned.
- Illustrations/examples of application of the Yuktis is given by the author of Arthaśāstra itself along with the definitions. Further, other examples from various disciplines that agree to

25 Consult Appendix 3 for a comparative table of available list of Yuktis

the definitions to, demonstrate the suitability of application of the devices in various fields will also be provided.

It could be observed that of the thirty-two devices presented in the Arthaśāstra

- 11 Yuktis are for Developing Scholarly Content creation
- 12 Yuktis are for structure the text/thesis
- 9 Yuktis are for polishing Language

It is important to note that the above classification is based on the definitions of the Yuktis used in this treatise – from Arthaśāstra. If there are other definitions from other sources, the category of any given Yuktis might change.

Though all the three aspects of Content, structure and Language are important for a well-rounded thesis or work of research, still this order is chosen obviously to indicate the decreasing order of priority for research purposes.

This order may prove as a useful criterion during both the construction and also evaluation of a work of research.

The sequencing of the Yuktis in the exposition below is done based on current day research requirements. This is different from the sequence provided in Arthaśāstra. The text Arthaśāstra does not provide any rationale behind the sequencing of the Yukti. Probably it follows an earlier set convention.

INSIGHTS

Definition of Tantrayuktis (Taṇṭiravutti) in Nannūl a 14th Century Tamil text that brings out its functions as well

நூல் பொருள் வழக்கு ஒடு வாய்ப்பக்காட்டி
nūl pŏruḷ vaḻakku ŏṭu vāyppakkāṭṭi
ஏற்புழி அறிந்து இதற்கு இவ்வகையாமென
eṟpuḻi aṟintu itaṟku ivvakaiyāmĕṉa
தகும் வகை செலுத்துதல் தந்திர உத்தி
takum vakai cĕluttutal tantira utti

(Reference: Nannūl, Potuppāyiram Verse 15)

Taṇṭiravutti (Tantrayuktis) is the practice that ensures that the subject of a work aligns with commonly accepted beliefs and the views of respected authors. It involves carefully judging and selecting appropriate topics based on this alignment.

Yuktis for Developing Scholarly Content

(11 Yuktis)

In every thesis, the imperative for unique and quality content is paramount. Originality ensures that the research contributes new insights or perspectives to the academic discourse, avoiding redundancy and advancing the collective understanding of the subject matter. Quality content, on the other hand, ensures that the research is rigorous, credible, and impactful. It involves thorough literature reviews, robust methodologies, and meticulous analysis, all aimed at producing findings that are both reliable and relevant. Unique and quality content not only demonstrates the researcher's expertise and intellectual contribution but also serves as a foundation for future scholarship. By offering fresh insights and addressing gaps in existing knowledge, such content enriches the academic community and inspires further research and innovation. Therefore, the integration of unique and quality content in any thesis is essential for its significance, credibility, and lasting impact. The following are the 11 devices of Tantrayuktis that can be considered to contribute towards creation of the unique and quality content in any given treatise. They are as follows –

- **1.**संशयः[26]– Doubt!
- **2-3** अनुमतम्, अपदेशः [27]–acceptance of views of others/quoting other's views (literary review)
- **4.** हेत्वर्थः[28] – (root)Cause/core area/crux
- **5-10.** उपदेशः, एकान्तः, नियोगः, अपवर्गः, विकल्प-समुच्चयौ [29]– suggestion/ Mandatory prescription/ Phenomenon without exceptions/ Generalizations with exceptions/optional rules/ combination of factors (based on observation and experiment)
- **11.** ऊह्यम् – Determinable facts!

Each of these are discussed in detail henceforth with definition from Kauṭilya Arthaśāstra and illustrations (primarly from Kauṭilya Arthaśāstra) and discussions and obsercations based on that.

26 saṃśaya
27 Anumata and Apadeśaḥ
28 Hetvārtha
29 Upadeśa, Ekāntaḥ, Niyogaḥ, Apavarga, Vikalpa and Samuccayau

1. संशयः Saṃśaya

Definition -

उभयतो हेतुमान् अर्थः संशयः।[30]

[31]*When the statement of reason is equally applicable to two kinds of circumstances, it is termed as doubt.*

Illustration -

...क्षीणलुब्धप्रकृतिम् अपचितप्रकृतिं वा[32] (Kauṭilya Arthaśāstra 7.5)

When there are two assailable enemies, one of virtuous character and under worse troubles, and another of vicious character, under less troubles, and with disloyal subjects, which of them is to be marched against first?

Let us understand the thought process behind the Yuktis in the context of Arthaśāstra. In the very beginning of the text the subject matter of Arthaśāstra was stated as –

पृथिव्या लाभे पालने च यावन्त्यर्थशास्त्राणि... [33](Kauṭilya Arthaśāstra 1.10)

---

30 ubhayato hetumān arthaḥ saṃśayaḥ.

31 Translations of the definition of the yuktis are based on the Translation of R.Shamashatry, 1929 Edition, Mysore Printing and Publishing house.

32 kṣīṇalubdhaprakṛtim apacitaprakṛtiṃ vā

33 pṛthivyā lābhe pālane ca yāvantyarthaśāstrāṇi..."

[34]This Arthaśāstra or Science of Polity has been made as a compendium of almost all those Arthaśāstras which, as a guidance to kings in acquiring and maintaining the earth...

From this it becomes evident that subject matter of Arthaśāstra is acquiring and maintaining earth/land/country. The example provided for the Saṃśaya Tantrayuktis, if one observes is connected to attain/acquire new earth/country – by attacking another kingdom.

Notes and Observations

As has been demonstrated from the above example, doubt is not on any random subject. It should be in such a manner that it furthers the development of insights, methods and approaches that are intimately connected to main subject matter.[35]

Take Aways

For a Researcher:

1. Develop a solid Research Doubt/question

For Evaluators:

1. Look for the content and nature of the research question that the researcher has taken up to address.

---

34 It has been observed that the translation of the illustrations in the respective chapters (for example in the current context 1.10) by Shamashastry is better than the translation of the illustrations given in the Tantrayukti section (adhikaraṇa 15). Hence careful choice of translation from Shamastry's work has been made to make illustrations more intelligible.

35 Kauṭilya does not merely expresss the doubt. He responds to it also as follows in the next line (7.5). *"When the enemy of virtuous character and under worse troubles is attacked, his subjects will help him; whereas, the subjects of the other of vicious character and under less troubles will be indifferent. Disloyal or indifferent subjects will endeavour to destroy even a strong king. Hence the conqueror should march against that enemy whose subjects are disloyal."*

2. अपदेशः Apadeśa

Definition -

एवम् असौ आह इति अपदेशः।[36]

Such a statement as "He says thus" is a quotation.

Illustration -

मन्त्रिपरिषदं द्वदशामात्यान् कुर्वीत इति मानवाः षोडशेति बार्हस्पत्याः, विंशतिमित्यौशनसाः, यथासामर्थ्यमिति कौटिल्यः।

(Kauṭilya Arthaśāstra 1.15)[37]

The school of Manu says that the assembly of ministers (mantripariṣad) shall be made to consist of twelve members. The school of Bṛhaspati says that it shall consist of sixteen members. The school of Uśanas says that it shall consist of twenty members. But Kauṭilya holds that it shall consist of as many members as the needs of his dominion require.

In determining the number of ministers in the council of ministers, the author of the Arthaśāstra has used Apadeśa TantraYukti. It is interesting to note that, before placing his view as "yathāsāmarthyam," Kauṭilya

36 evam asau āha iti apadeśaḥ. -

37 mantripariṣadaṃ dvadaśāmātyān kurvīta iti mānavāḥ ṣoḍaśeti bārhaspatyāḥ, viṃśatimityauśanasāḥ, yathāsāmarthyamiti kauṭilyaḥ. mantrādhikāraḥ (arthaśā 1.15)

carefully notes and quotes the views of other schools of thought on this point. This is a Yuktis for developing scholarly content, as only that content is original or unique which is generated after considering the existing views on a given issue or question.

Notes and Observations

1. Let us first think about the conection of this Yuktis with the previous one. When a doubt or question arises one should not run a conclusion that occurs to one's mind. In methodical research one has look for the views of others on the same issue. Hence Apadeśa has been placed after Saṃśaya. It is to be noted that this sequence of Yuktis is entire by the author of this book and not ancient authors. Hence the examples will also not have continuity. But this is the obvious when we think methodically.
2. Further, a researcher should have done an extensive survey of all accessible sources before theorizing or presenting his views – only then he will be able to freely quote. Quotations from various sources above, point to that. It is to be noted that at the very beginning of the text Arthaśāstra Kauṭilya states

पृथिव्या लाभे पालने च यावन्त्यर्थशास्त्राणि पूर्वाचार्यैः प्रस्थापितानि
प्रायशस्तानि संहृत्यैककमिदमर्थशास्त्रं कृतम्।

(Kauṭilya Arthaśāstra 1.1).

This Arthaśāstra or Science of Polity has been made as a compendium of almost all those Arthaśāstras which, as a guidance to kings in acquiring and maintaining the earth, have been composed by ancient teachers.

As could be noted from the underlined portion – the word "all" – indicates the effort put in by the author to consult extensively pre-existing treatises on the subject. The usage "almost" is also crucial from the point view of research. As is the best practice, the author exhibits the possible limitations of his literary survey. There might be some texts which may not have come to light or inaccessible, at the time of composition of the present work. All those sources are accounted for by the term "almost".

3. The very arrangement of the quotes in the illustration are worth noting. The quotes are presented in the ascending order of the number of ministers suggested by previous authors in the subject from twelve to twenty. This indicates that meticulous approach in organizing the quotes. This shows that it is not some haphazard collection of views on the topic of discussion. The collected quotes should be sequenced on some logic. It could be chronological order or it could be based on the numerical value that the quotes may contain which could either be in the ascending or descending order as may be required or any other such valid reasoning. Kauṭilya implies that collection of references and organizing them following a logic will facilitate better analysis. This is very useful research cutting across subjects and time.
4. Finally, in the illustration above, by juxtaposing his view at the end with the quotes of others, Kauṭilya expresses the universal applicability of his own views – in comparison to the view of other who merely fix a particular number for the council. Here Kauṭilya teaches the very purpose of quoting pre-existing views on a matter under consideration. In a thesis, Implicitly or explicitly, the researcher should express his views in relation to the quotes that he/she has given. Otherwise Quoting the views of others should be merely considered as an effort to fill-up pages. The examiners of a thesis can understand quality of thesis writing by looking into this aspect.

Take Aways

For a Researcher:

1. Conduct In-depth Literature Review: Ensure your literature review is exhaustive, encompassing diverse and pertinent sources.

2. Arrange References Coherently: Organize your references in a coherent structure to enhance reader comprehension and accessibility.
3. Integrate your assessment with Quotations: Seamlessly blend your perspectives with quoted sources, establishing a coherent relationship and comparative analysis.

For Evaluators:

1. Asses the extent of Literature Review whether it is extensive or minimal
2. Note whether the References are organized in a Logical manner
3. Observe whether the researcher has juxtaposed his Views with the quoted views.

3. अनुमतम् Anumata

Definition -

परवाक्यमप्रतिषिद्धम् अनुमतम्।[38]

When the opinion of another person is stated, but not refuted, it is acceptance of that opinion.

Illustration -

पक्षावुरस्यं प्रतिग्रहः इत्यौशनसो व्यूहविभागः[39]

(Kauṭilya Arthaśāstra 10.3).

Wings, front and reserve is the form of an array of the army according to the school of Uśanas[40].

As evident from the example, Kauṭilya quotes and accepts the view of Uśanas in the array of Army (vyūha).

Examples from other texts

1. In Aṣṭādhyāyī we see many occasions where the anumata Tantrayuktis is used. A few examples are as follows - [41]लोपः

38 paravākyamapratiṣiddham anumatam.

39 pakṣāvurasyaṃ pratigrahaḥ ityauśanaso vyūhavibhāgaḥ

40 Usanas – Shukracharya

41 lopaḥ śākalyasya (8.3.19), avaṅ sphoṭāyanasya (6.1.123), oto gārgyasya (8.3.20)

शाकल्यस्य (8.3.19)[42], अवङ् स्फोटायनस्य (6.9.123)[43], ओतो गार्ग्यस्य (8.3.20)[44] - As evident Pāṇini has quoted the views of grammarian known to him like śākalya, sphoṭāyana and Gārgya.

2. Vātsyāyana's Commentary to Nyāyasūtra-bhāṣya

इन्द्रियस्य वै सतः मनसः इन्द्रियेभ्यः पृथगुपदेशो धर्मभेदत्।...।
मनसश्चेन्द्रियभावात् तन्न
वाच्यं लक्षणान्तरमिति। तन्त्रान्तरसमाचाराच्चैतत् प्रत्येतव्यम्।
परमतमप्रतिषिद्धमनुमतमिति हि तन्त्रयुक्तिः।[45] (1.4)

The context of Utilization of Tantrayuktis in Nyāyasūtra-bhāṣya is as follows: the fourth Sūtra of Nyāyasūtra definies the direct perception (Pratyakṣa) caused by sense organs. While discussing this Vātsyāyana, the commentator states that mind is also a sense organ. Therefore, the knowledge caused by the Manas is also direct perception. The definition of direct perception (Pratyakṣa) by the sense organs applies to the knowledge that arises out of Manas too.

Vātsyāyana follows it up with a statement to remove a doubt. It is as follows -since there is no direct mention of Manas being a sense organ in the Sūtra-s of Gautama, how can the definition of the direct preception arising from sense organs be applied to the Manas?' Vātsyāyana sets it at rest, stating that though there is no direct reference in the Sūtra-s of the Gautama regarding this issue, the view of other schools of thought on Manas being a sense organ can be taken to be the view of Gautama also. TantraYukti Anumata authorises such an interpretation. The definition of anuamta is - *The view of the other (author/scholar/school of thought),*

---

42 व् and य् preceded by अ or आ and the end of a पद are elided before an अश् letter (vowels and soft-consonants) according the opinion of śākalya।

43 According to the opinion of sphoṭāyana, there is the substitution of अवङ् for the ओ of गो when it is followed by any vowel.

44 य् preceded by ओ is elided before an अश् letter (vowels and soft-consonants) according the opinion of gārgya.

45 indriyasya vai sataḥ manasaḥ indriyebhyaḥ pṛthagupadeśo dharmabhedat... manasaścendriyabhāvāttanna vācyaṃ lakṣaṇāntaramiti. tantrāntarasamācāràccaitat pratyetavyam. paramatamapratiṣiddhamanumatamiti hi tantrayuktiḥ.

on a particular issue, not refuted by another author in his text amounts to the acceptence of the view of the former.

Applying this rule, Vātsyāyana states that it can be assumed that Gautama agrees with the view of others to the effect that mind is a sense organ.

The Sankhya Sūtra-s, which accroding to Maxmuller[46] are the last arrangement of the doctrines accumlated in one philosophical school during centuries of Paramparā or tradition, clearly states that mind is a sense organ.

3. Ācārya śaṅkara's Brahmasūtra-bhāṣya: Acharya Śaṅkara accepts the framework of Yogaśāstra with regard to determining the divisions of Prāṇa, by utilizing the services of Anumata Tantrayuktis –

एवं तर्हि 'परमतमप्रतिषिद्धमनुमतं भवति' इति न्यायात् इहापि योगशास्त्रप्रसिद्धा मनसः पञ्च वृत्तयः परिगृह्यन्ते।[47] (2.4.12)

*Then in that case, following the maxim 'An opinion of even an opponent which is not objected to, may, when necessary, be adopted', the five-fold modes of the mind known in the science of Yoga, viz. 'Right knowledge, error; imagination, slumber and memory' (*Pātañjala *Yogasūtra 1.1.6), may be accepted here.*

Notes and Observations

1. Utility of Systematic Literature Review: - Systematic literature reviews allow the collected material to be used in various ways. Quoted views can either be accepted or rejected. If a quoted view is neither rejected nor countered with a different view, it is considered accepted. Consequently, defending the unrejected quotation becomes the researcher's responsibility.

46 The Six systems of Indian Philosophy, Max Muller, Read Books, 2007, p.220

47 evaṃ tarhi 'paramatamapratiṣiddhamanumataṃ bhavati' iti nyāyāt ihāpi yogaśāstraprasiddhā manasaḥ pañca vṛttayaḥ parigṛhyante|

2. Acknowledgment of Sources: - It is crucial to acknowledge the source of quoted views to avoid plagiarism. Plagiarism, which is the use of others' views without giving credit, has several pitfalls:

    - It is a dishonest practice, even if unintentional, as research is based on truth and originality.
    - It wastes time and resources, adding nothing new to the field of knowledge.

3. Pāṇiniyan convention of Optional Acceptance: - In Pāṇiniyan convention, views of others that are presented but not explicitly rejected are optionally accepted. This means that non-rejection does not imply that the quoted view is the only correct view but that it may coexist with the author's view. This flexibility allows the author to use Tantrayuktis to fully or optionally accept others' views.
4. Dynamic and Robust Knowledge Exchange: - The examples from Nyāyasūtra-bhāṣya and Brahmasūtra-bhāṣya demonstrate the dynamic and robust relationship between different systems of knowledge in exchanging views. This reflects the intellectual integrity and methodological sophistication in constructing theses in Indian Knowledge systems.
5. Creation of Useful Content: - This Yukti, which involves quoting and accepting others' views, helps in creating useful content for a thesis by being aware of similar views or frameworks available in other parallel knowledge systems and authors. This methodological approach enriches the thesis with a broader perspective and deeper understanding.

Take Aways

For a Researcher:

1. Utilize systematic literature reviews effectively and justify quotations left unchallenged.

2. Ensure thorough acknowledgment of all sources to prevent plagiarism and showcase originality.
3. Verify adherence to the Pāṇiniyan tradition of presenting views without explicit rejection, suggesting potential acceptance.
4. Integrate perspectives from diverse knowledge systems dynamically to uphold intellectual integrity.
5. Craft valuable content by incorporating analogous viewpoints and frameworks from alternative systems of knowledge.

For Evaluators:

Based on the above inputs following points can be looked into by the thesis evaluators -

1. Assess how the researcher utilizes systematic literature reviews and defends unrejected quotations.
2. Ensure all sources are properly acknowledged to avoid plagiarism and demonstrate originality.
3. Check for the Pāṇiniyan approach of presenting views without explicit rejection, indicating optional acceptance.
4. Look for dynamic integration of views from various knowledge systems.

4. हेत्वर्थः Hetvarthaḥ

Definition -

हेतुः अर्थसाधकः हेत्वर्थः।[48]

What is meant to prove an assertion is the purport of reason

Illustration -

अर्थमूलौ हि धर्मकामौ। (हि हेतुसूचकम्)
(अर्थ एव प्रधान इति कौटिल्यः।)[49]

(Kauṭilya Arthaśāstra 1.7)

For charity(Dharma) and enjoyment(Kāma) of life depend upon wealth

Hetu and artha are the two components in this Yukti. Hetu is the cause and artha is the purpose. The purpose (artha) in the above illustration is - अर्थ एव प्रधान इति कौटिल्यः - to establish the supremacy of Artha (wealth over Dharma and Kāma) and the hetu (cause) provided is अर्थमूलौ हि धर्मकामौ It is indeed a very sound cause as nothing can be achieved without wealth.

48 hetuḥ arthasādhakaḥhetvarthaḥ.

49 arthamūlau hi dharmakāmau. (hi hetusūcakam) – (arthaśā 1.7) (artha eva pradhāna iti kauṭilyaḥ.)

Notes and observation

In Saṃskṛta there is a famous statement - न केवला हि प्रतिज्ञा प्रतिज्ञातमर्थं साधयेत्। [50] It's important to note that simply stating claims without evidence does not establish their validity. While conducting research, various propositions may come to mind, reflecting active thinking. However, merely mentioning these propositions without providing supporting evidence, references, and inferences renders them hollow. It's crucial for every claim to be substantiated with evidence, whether epistemological, linguistic, logical, or empirical, depending on the nature of the claim. This ensures that the content of the work is logical and sound.

Take Aways

For a Researcher:

1. Substantiate Every Claim: Ensure that each claim made in your thesis is supported by evidence, references, and inferences to avoid hollow assertions.
2. Utilize Various Forms of Substantiation: Back up your claims with epistemological, linguistic, logical, or empirical evidence, depending on the nature of the claim, to enhance the logical and sound quality of your work.

For Evaluators:

Assess for Substantiation for Every Assertion. Require that each claim presented in the thesis is supported by evidence, references, and inferences to ensure its validity and credibility.

---

50 na kevalā hi pratijñā pratijñātamarthaṃ sādhayet.

5. एकान्तः Ekānta

Definition -

सर्वत्र आयत्तम् एकान्तः। [51]

That which is universal in its application is conclusion or an established fact

Illustration -

तस्मादुत्थानमात्मनः कुर्वीत"[52]

(Kauṭilya Arthaśāstra 1.19)

Hence the king shall ever be wakeful.

This chapter is on Rājapraṇidhi. It states the attitude and duties of the king. Prior to the statement given as an illustration above, the section states: *"If a king is energetic, his subjects will be equally energetic. If he is reckless, they will not only be reckless likewise, but also eat into his works. Besides, a reckless king will easily fall into the hands of his enemies"* (Shamashastry). *"Hence, a king shall ever be wakeful."* In the context of the Arthaśāstra, this is a truly universal rule. As long as a person is a king, he should be wakeful. No exceptions can be made in that regard.

51 sarvatra āyattam ekāntaḥ.

52 tasmādutthānamātmanaḥ kurvīta

Example from other texts

Let us consider and example from Suśruta-saṃhitā (6.65.23) -

त्रिवृत् विरेचयति मदनफलं वामयत्येव।[53]

The Trivṛt, without exception, leads to a purgative laxative effect, and the Madanaphala, without exception, leads to vomiting.

Notes and observations

This method assists authors in expressing their views on phenomena with a high level of certainty, indicating prolonged and repeated observations rather than vague or ambiguous statements. Such confident assertions, backed by proper justifications, signify the quality of the work. Researchers are advised not to rush to conclusions but rather repeat experiments under various conditions, observe patiently over time, or widen their survey of occurrences to reach firm conclusions. These qualities are invaluable for researchers, and the validity or time-tested nature of their work depends on such well-studied observations. Statements demonstrating the spirit of this method should be recognized as indications of diligent work by the author.

Take Aways

For a Researcher:

1. Express Certainty in Observations: When stating views on phenomena, aim for a high level of certainty, indicating prolonged and repeated observations rather than ambiguous statements.
2. Avoid Hasty Conclusions
3. Back Assertions with Justifications: Ensure that confident assertions are backed by proper justifications, indicating the quality and thoroughness of your work.

---

53 trivṛt virecayati madanaphalaṃ vāmayatyeva.

For Evaluators:

Evaluate the **level of certainty expressed** in observations, looking for indications of prolonged and repeated observations rather than ambiguous and hasty statements and observations.

6. नियोगः Niyoga

Definition -

एवं नान्यथा इति नियोगः[54]

Thus, and not otherwise' is command

Illustration -

नवबुद्धिर्यदुच्यते तच्छास्त्रोपदेशमिवाभिजानाति।
तस्माद्धर्मर्थञ्च अस्य उपदिशेत् नाधर्ममनर्थं च।[55]

(Kauṭilya Arthaśāstra 1.17)

(Just as a fresh object is stained with whatever it is brought in close association, so a prince with fresh mind is apt to regard as scientific injunctions all that he is told of.) Hence, he shall be taught only of righteousness and of wealth (artha), but not of unrighteousness and of non-wealth

This is an injunction which is inviolable or not to be done otherwise. The example is given from the context of upbringing of a prince. The mind of a young prince will be fresh. Hence nothing unrighteous should be taught - only righteous. Such a prince will grow up to an asset and not a thorn in the flesh for the king.

---

54 evaṃ nānyathā iti niyogaḥ

55 navabuddhiryaducyate tacchāsstropadeśamivābhijānāti.) tasmāddharmarthañca asya upadiśet nādharmamanarthaṃ ca. (arthaśā 1.17)

Example from other texts

पथ्यमेव भोक्तव्यम्।[56]

(suśruta-saṃhitā uttara-tantra 65.37)

One should strictly follow dietery regulation

This example is a command which should not be violated. The example in the context of Ekānta observes the unchanging phenomena of working of certain herbs whereas this is of the nature injunction that should not be violated.

Notes and observations

Going by Kauṭilya 's view there only seems to be a slight difference between Ekānta and Niyoga, whereas Ekānta seems to be an observation on phenomena without exception, niyoga is connected with prescriptive injunction which shall not be done otherwise. Towards creating original content – this Yuktis give input to a researcher on how to state a command/prescription that should not be violated.

But as observable from the example for Suśruta-saṃhitā – this Yuktis is seen as an unviolable rule and does not emphasize on the method of doing it. This also brings out the fact that Yuktis is seen in different light by different authours of the past. This opens up the possibility of further work in the field of Tantrayuktis towards consolidating all possible shades of meaning of a given Yukti.

Take Aways

As there is only a slight difference between the previous and this Yukti, the observations for researchers and evaluators of research remain the same.

56 pathyameva bhoktavyam.

7. उपदेशः Upadeśa

Definition -

एवं वर्तितव्यमिति उपदेशः।[57]

Such statement as "Thus one should live," is guidance

Illustration -

धर्मार्थाविरोधेन कामं सेवेत। न निस्सुखः स्यात्।[58]

(Kauṭilya Arthaśāstra 1.7)

Not violating the laws of righteousness and economy, he should live.

The example statement is from the Rājarṣivṛtta- The Life of a Saintly King. Unlike Niyoga which is a command which cannot be violated - this is beneficial guidance, advice.

Example from other Texts

"तथा न जागृयाद्रात्रौ दिवास्वप्नं च वर्जयेत्।"

(suśruta-saṃhitā uttara-tantra 65.14)[59]

This example is given by Suśruta for this Tantrayuktis. As can be seen in this case - waking at night and not sleeping during day is not an

57 evaṃ vartitavyamiti upadeśaḥ.

58 dharmārthāvirodhena kāmaṃ seveta. na nissukhaḥ syāt. (arthaśā 1.7)

59 "tathā na jāgṛyādrātrau divāsvapnaṃ ca varjeyet." (Su sam. uttara 65.14)

inviolable rule. But a beneficial advice. Sometimes one has to wake during nights and sleep during days for specific tasks. But in normal course of life the following this teaching would be beneficial.

Notes and Observations

A researcher gets to know another kind of observation that is possible out of research. Not all observations need to be an unchallengeable command at all conditions. Here it is in the form of a guidance if generally adhered to will be beneficial.

Take Aways

For a Researcher:

As a researcher not all your findings need to be ground breaking. An advice on doing things in a certain beneficial way, suggested based on experimentation and keen observation is also a new contribution.

For Evaluators:

Acknowledge that not all findings must be revolutionary. Insights and recommendations derived from careful experimentation and observation are also valuable contributions to the field.

8. अपवर्गः Apavarga

Definition -

अभिप्लुतव्यपकर्षणम् अपवर्गः।[60]

Removal of an undesired implication from a statement is exception

Illustration -

नित्यम् आसन्नमरिबलम् वासयेद् अन्यत्र अभ्यन्तरकोपशङ्कया।[61]

(Kauṭilya Arthaśāstra 9.2)

A king may allow his enemy's army to be present close to his territory, unless he suspects of the existence of any internal trouble.

The rule here is a king can always allow his enemy army to stay close to his borders, but not if there is a possibility/doubt of internal strife. It is possible that if there is any internal strife and the instability closer inside the kingdom, then the opponent can take advantage and unseat the king by rushing in his army which is stationed near the border. When there is such a possibility of civil strife, it is implied that such an enemy army should be engaged elsewhere and not close to his borders.

60 abhiplutavyapakarṣaṇam apavargaḥ.

61 nityam āsannamaribalam vāsayed anyatra abhyantarakopaśaṅkayā. (arthaśā 9.2)

Example from other texts

अस्वेद्या विषोपसृष्टा अन्यत्र कीटविषाद्।[62]

(suśruta-saṃhitā 6.65.18)

Fomentation should not be applied to persons suffering from the effects of poisoning excepting those suffering from insect poisoning.

Here the pervasive observation is- prohibition of fomentation to those suffering from effects of poisoning. The Apavarga – exception is insect poisoning. For insect poisoning fomentation can be applied.

Notes and Observations

The concept of a pervasive rule and its exceptions is crucial in any field of knowledge. Through observation and experimentation, researchers establish rules, but they must also identify exceptions. Noting these exceptions helps to understand how the rule applies under different conditions and situations. Mentioning exceptions demonstrates that the researcher has thoroughly tested the rule in various contexts, repeatedly. This process leads to the creation of valid content.

Take Aways

For a Researcher:

1. When creating rules based on your research, always identify and note any exceptions.
2. Ensure that you test the application of rules under various conditions and situations.

For Evaluators:

1. Ensure the thesis includes identification and documentation of any exceptions to the established rules.
2. Verify that the thesis shows evidence of testing the rules across different conditions and scenarios.

---

62 asvedyā viṣopasṛṣṭā anyatra kīṭaviṣād. (suśrutasaṃhitā 6.65.18)

9. समुच्चयः Samuccaya

Definition -

अनेन चानेन चेति।[63]

Combining homogenous ideas and stating together

Illustration -

स्व-जातः पितुर्बन्धूनां च दायादः... [64]

(Kauṭilya Arthaśāstra 3.7.13)

A natural son can claim ***relationship*** *both with his father and his father's relatives; (but a son born to another man/adopted can have relationship only with his adopter.)*

It is essential to determine who can claim relationship to a person and his relatives and thereby have a say in the property inheritance. Hence the above sentence. Samuccaya happens here when relationship of a son is clubbed with both father and his relatives. Whereas for an adoptee relationshiop/kinship is limted only to the father who has adopted him and not with the relatives of the father.

63 anena cānena ceti

64 sva-jātaḥ piturbandhūnāṃ ca dāyādaḥ… (K.A 03.7.13)

Example from other texts

इह खलु वर्णश्च स्वरश्च गन्धश्च रसश्च स्पर्शश्च चक्षुश्च श्रोत्रं च घ्राणं च रसनं च स्पर्शनं च सत्त्वं च भक्तिश्च शौचं च शीलंचाचारश्च स्मृतिश्चाकृतिश्च प्रकृतिश्च विकृतिश्च बलं च ग्लानिश्च मेधा च हर्षश्च रौक्ष्यं च स्नेहश्च तन्द्रा चारम्भश्च गौरवं चलाघवं च गुणाश्चाहारश्च विहारश्चाहारपरिणामश्चोपायश्चापायश्च व्याधिश्च व्याधिपूर्वरूपं च वेदनाश्चोपद्रवाश्च च्छाया चप्रतिच्छाया च स्वप्नदर्शनं च दूताधिकारश्च पथि चौत्पातिकं चातुरकुले भावावस्थान्तराणि च भेषजसंवृत्तिश्च भेषजविकारयुक्तिश्चेति परीक्ष्याणि प्रत्यक्षानुमानोपदेशैरायुषः प्रमाणावशेषं जिज्ञासमानेन भिषजा|| [65]

(caraka-saṃhitā 5.1.3)

The following entities should be examined by the physician desiring to assess the residual span of life of the patient using direct observation, and inference such as: Physical appearance (complexion, appearance of eyes, ears, nose, tongue, skin), including attributes perceived by the senses (voice, smell, taste, touch, etc.) Behavioral traits (mood, upkeep, conduct, etc.) Dietary habits and lifestyle (regimens, ability to digest, etc.) Existing health conditions (signs of diseases, symptoms, complications, drug use, effect of medicines on illness and on the patient) Bad omens perceived by the physician on his way to patient's house, changed conditions of the patient's residence, signs and symptoms indicating the residual span of life may be evident on these factors. Hence physician should pay careful attention to each one of

---

65 iha khalu varṇaśca svaraśca gandhaśca rasaśca sparśaśca cakṣuśca śrotraṃ ca ghrāṇaṃ ca rasanaṃ ca sparśanaṃ ca sattvaṃ ca bhaktiśca śaucaṃ ca śīlaṃcācāraśca smṛtiścākṛtiśca prakṛtiśca vikṛtiśca balaṃ ca glāniśca medhā ca harṣaścaraukṣyaṃ ca snehaśca tandrā cārambhaśca gauravaṃ calāghavaṃ ca guṇāścāhāraśca vihāraścāhārapariṇāmaścopāyaścāpāyaśca vyādhiśca vyādhipūrvarūpaṃ ca vedanāścopadravāśca cchāyā capraticchāyā ca svapnadarśanaṃ ca dūtādhikāraśca pathi cautpātikaṃ cāturakule bhāvāvasthāntarāṇi ca bheṣajasaṃvṛttiśca bheṣajavikārayuktiśceti parīkṣyāṇi pratyakṣānumānopadeśairāyuṣaḥ pramāṇāvaśeṣaṃ jijñāsamānena bhiṣajā|| (carakasaṃhitā 5.1.3)

them and interpretation should be made based on his observations, knowledge and scriptural advice.[66]

Notes and Observations

This Yuktis is somewhat similar to the previous Yuktis in the context of being thorough going. Here as can be seen from the examples all aspects that are to be examined are pooled together missing out nothing. This is essential for a complete treatment of a content under consideration. An incomplete advice or content serves no ones purpose. The quality of the content is determined by its completeness including as many factors as possible.

This shows the importance of being focussed on the details – compiling and collating all possible information pertaining to any given aspect of study and research.

Take Aways

For a Researcher:

Pool together all relevant aspects to avoid missing any important details. Pay meticulous attention to detail and compile comprehensive information to provide a holistic treatment of the subject matter.

For Evaluators:

Verify that the thesis thoroughly whether it addresses all relevant aspects, demonstrating meticulous attention to detail and compiling comprehensive information for a holistic treatment of the subject matter.

66 Source of Translation: https://www.carakasamhitaonline.com/index.php/Varnasvariyam_Indriyam_Adhyaya

Yuktis for Developing Scholarly Content

10. विकल्पः Vikalpa

optional rule

Definition -

अनेन वा अनेन वेति विकल्पः।[67]

Either with this or that

Illustration -

(रिक्थं पुत्रवतः पुत्रा) दुहितरो वा धर्मिष्ठेषु विवाहेषु जाताः

(Kauṭilya Arthaśāstra 3.5)

Or daughters born of approved marriage (dharmavivàha)

The above example is about inheritance of property especially the immovable property (riktahm). Those whose have sons or his daughters, born out of approved marriage can inherit the immoveable property of the father. The optionality of either the Son or the daughter having a right over inheritance is aspect being illustrated by Kauṭilya.

67 anena vā anena veti vikalpaḥ.

Example from other Texts

सारोदकं वाऽथ कुशोदकं वा मधूदकं वा त्रिफलारसं वा
सोधुं पिबेद्वा निगदं प्रमेही माध्वीकमग्र्यं चिरसंस्थितं वा[68]

(caraka-saṃhitā 6.6.46)

The patient suffering from prameha should drink sārodaka (water boiled with the heartwood of khadira, etc.), kuśodaka (water boiled with kuśa), madhūdaka (water mixed with honey), triphalā rasa (juice or decoction of triphalā), Śodhu (a type of wine that is properly fermented), or mādhvika (another type of wine of superior quality prepared after fermenting for a long time).

Notes and Observations

As can be observed from both examples, more than one option is presented for the question under discussion. This indicates the exploration and experimentation undertaken by the researcher on various options to address the same issue. It highlights the level of investigation done by the researcher, who has identified multiple solutions for a given problem.

Viklapa Tantrayukti has been extensively used across systems of knowledge in ancient India. In Pāṇini Aṣṭādhyāyī also we find various sūtras that use the Vikalpa Eg: पारे मध्ये षष्ठ्या वा (2.1.18[69]. Even in Yogasūtras we have the concept of using optional rules/methods (Vikalpa) For example in Yoga-sūtra- ईश्वरप्रणिधानद् वा (Ys 1.23)[70], प्रच्छर्दनविधारणाभ्यां वा प्राणस्य (१.३४)[71] can be seen as examples of optional rule.

---

68 sārodakaṃ vā›tha kuśodakaṃ vā madhūdakaṃ vā triphalārasaṃ vā śodhuṃ sodhuṃ pibedvā nigadaṃ pramehī mādhvīkamagryaṃ cirasaṃsthitaṃ vā (carakasaṃ 6.6.46)

69 pāre madhye ṣaṣṭhyā vā

70 īśvarapraṇidhānad vā

71 pracchardanavidhāraṇābhyāṃ vā prāṇasya

Take Aways

For a Researcher:

Explore and experiment with various options to address the same issue, demonstrating thorough investigation and presenting multiple solutions.

For Evaluators:

Verify that the thesis demonstrates a thorough exploration of various options and solutions for the issue at hand, reflecting extensive research and experimentation.

11. ऊह्यम् Ūhya

Definition -

अनुक्तकरणम् ऊह्यम्[72]

That which is to be determined after consideration is determinable fact;

Illustration -

यावद्दाता प्रतिग्रहीता च नोपहतौ स्याताम्,
तथानुशयं कुशलाः कल्पयेयुः।[73]

(Kauṭilya Arthaśāstra 3.16)

Experts shall determine the validity or invalidity of gifts so that neither the giver nor the receiver is likely to be hurt thereby.

It is interesting to note that how of rescission (revoking the validity of the gift) is not specified. But it left to the descrition of the experts to evaluate the situation and decide. This is Ūhyam, where the specifics are to be determined in each and every case and only general guidelines can be provided.

72 anuktakaraṇam ūhyam

73 yāvaddātā pratigrahītā ca nopahatau syātām,
tathānuśayaṃ kuśalāḥ kalpayeyuḥ. (arthaśā 3.16)

Example from other texts

ऊह्यं नाम यदनिबद्धं ग्रन्थे प्रज्ञया तर्क्यत्वेनोपदिश्यते;
यथा- "परिसङ्ख्यातमपि यद्यद् द्रव्यमयौगिकं मन्येत तत्तदपकर्षयेत्" [74] इति

(āyurvedadīpikā (caraka-saṃhitā) 8.12.44)

The logical interpretation of given text for better understanding is Ūhya. For example. while describing the (medicinal) material (which can be used for basti), it is advised that (a Vaidya) can exclude those not suitable (for a particular patient)

Notes and Observations

This is an interesting Yukti. Even in the most systematic disciplines of knowledge, certain things or phenomena cannot be predicted with final detail or perfection. However, provisions must still be made for them by a thorough researcher who aims to create useful content. Such possibilities must be noted and explicitly stated. This is evident from the two examples provided above. It highlights the depth of study required to create content that accounts for all possible details.

Take Aways

For a Researcher:

Acknowledge and document highly context-specific occurrences and details, ensuring that your research accounts for all possible outcomes.

For Evaluators:

Confirm that the thesis addresses highly context-specific possibilities and details, reflecting a thorough and detailed study.

---

74 ūhyaṃ nāma yadanibaddhaṃ granthe prajñayā tarkyatvenopadiśyate; yathā- "parisaṅkhyātamapi yadyad dravyamayaugikaṃ manyeta tattadapakarṣayet" (vi.a.8) iti

Summary

The following can be stated as summary about the Yuktis that were discussd with illustrations on creating unique, quality content in thesis –

1. **Structured Doubt:** Doubt should be structured and directed towards furthering insights and approaches related to the main subject matter. It serves as the foundation for original thinking and thesis development. (Saṃśaya)
2. **Comprehensive Literature Review and Logical Organization of Quotes:** Extensive literature review is essential before presenting views, allowing researchers to freely quote and substantiate their arguments. Quotes should be organized logically, indicating meticulous research and facilitating better analysis. This demonstrates a systematic approach to research across subjects and time. (Apadeśa)
3. **Universal Applicability of Views**: Researchers should juxtapose their views with those of others to express the universal applicability of their ideas. This demonstrates the purpose of quoting pre-existing views and enhances the quality of thesis writing. (Anumata)
4. **Substantiation of Claims**: Every claim should be backed up with substantiation, whether epistemological, linguistic, logical, or empirical. This ensures logical and sound content creation. (Hetvārtha)
5. **Observation and Experimentation**: Researchers should avoid jumping to conclusions and instead repeat experiments,

patiently observe, or conduct wide-ranging surveys to arrive at firm conclusions. This ensures the validity and time-testedness of the work. (Ekānta, Niyoga, Upadeśa)

6. **Thorough Examination and Exploration**: All aspects and options of a subject should be thoroughly examined and explored and compiled, leaving no room for incomplete advice or content. This indicates diligence and completeness in research. (Vikalpa and Samucaya)
7. **Acknowledgment of Exceptions and Provision for Uncertainty**: Exceptions to rules should be noted down, aiding in understanding the working of injunctions in various conditions and situations. Researchers should explicitly state possibilities that cannot be predicted with finality, demonstrating a thorough understanding of the subject matter and its nuances. (Apavarga, Ūhya)

Remarkably, these methodologies existed even before the Common Era, evident from the examples quoted from in ancient Indian texts like the Arthaśāstra, Pāṇini's Aṣṭādhyāyī. It was also illustrated that in the early years of Common era also texts like Suśruta-saṃhitā and Yogasūtras have utilized these inputs in their texts. This structured approach served as a strong scaffold for the emergence of numerous texts within the Indian knowledge system, endowing them with enduring relevance and contributing to the depth and breadth of understanding in various fields even today.

And as evident from the inputs, these can be equally utilized in the current day thesis construction practices across discipline to enhance th quality of the content. This brings out the utility of these thought processes even now.

ACTIVITY

Browse the web and find at least two articles for each of the Yuktis of this section from-

- Newspaper Opinion columns
- Scientific Research papers - https://www.ncbi.nlm.nih.gov/pubmed/
- Research papers across disciplines - https://www.academia.edu/
- https://www.researchgate.net/
- Write ups on culture - https://www.esamskriti.com/ https://www.indica.today/

Some questions for reflection and critical thinking

1. How can the principles of structured doubt be applied to your own research process? What steps can you take to ensure that doubt is directed towards furthering insights and approaches related to your main subject matter?
2. Reflect on your current literature review process. Are there any areas where you could improve the comprehensiveness and organization of your literature review? How might you enhance the logical organization of quotes to better support your arguments?
3. Consider the universal applicability of your own ideas and perspectives. In what ways do your views intersect with or diverge from those of others in your field? How might juxtaposing your views with those of others strengthen the quality of your thesis writing?
4. How do you currently substantiate claims in your research? Are there any types of substantiation (epistemological, linguistic, logical, empirical) that you tend to rely on more heavily? How might you diversify your approach to ensure logical and sound content creation?
5. Reflect on your approach to observation and experimentation. Are there any instances where you've been tempted to jump to conclusions prematurely? How might you incorporate the principles of patience and thoroughness to ensure the validity and time-testedness of your work?
6. Evaluate the thoroughness of your examination and exploration process. Are there any aspects or options of your subject that you've overlooked or not fully explored? How might you ensure diligence and completeness in your research moving forward?

7. Consider how you currently acknowledge exceptions and uncertainties in your research. Are there any areas where you've struggled to account for unpredictability or variability? How might explicitly stating possibilities that cannot be predicted with finality enhance your understanding of the subject matter and its nuances?

Yuktis for Structuring a Thesis

12 Yuktis

Structuring a thesis is paramount as it provides a cohesive framework for presenting research findings and arguments. A well-organized structure ensures clarity, coherence, and logical progression, guiding readers through complex ideas and evidence. By delineating chapters, sections, and sub-sections, a structured thesis facilitates comprehension and enhances readability. Moreover, it enables researchers to effectively convey their main points and contribute to scholarly discourse in a systematic manner. Additionally, a clear structure aids in the planning and execution of research, helping researchers stay focused and on track throughout the writing process. Ultimately, the need to structure a thesis lies in its ability to effectively communicate and disseminate knowledge.

It can be observed that 12 Yuktis from among the 32 Yuktis of Kauṭilya in Arthaśāstra contribute to structuring the thesis. The Yuktis are

1-2 अधिकरण विधाने[75] – Subject matter and Contents

3-4 उद्देश- निर्देशौ[76] – listing and elaborating

75 adhikaraṇa and vidhāna

76 uddeśa and nirdeśa

5-6 पूर्वपक्ष-उत्तरपक्षौ[77] – arranging arguments against and for topic under discussion (from another view, this may also be taken as pair of Yuktis that contribute to the core content of the work)

7-8 अतिक्रान्त-अनागतावेक्षणे[78] – Yuktis to help as to where to elaborate upon a specific topic – earlier or later

9-10-11 अतिदेश-प्रदेशौ, प्रसङ्गः [79] devices for Optimum utilization of arguments/elaborations

12 विपर्ययः [80] - stating a rule for a specific purpose and reversing the same rule to achieve it inverse

It is observable that mostly these neatly fall into pairs or sets. As done in the previous chapter these are discussed with definition, illustration (primarily from Kauṭilya Arthaśāstra) and discussions are carried out.

77 pūrvapakṣa and uttarapakṣa

78 atikrāntāvekṣaṇa and anāgatavekṣaṇa

79 atideśa pradeśa and prasaṅga

80 viparyaya

1. अधिकरणम् Adhikaraṇa

Definition -

यमर्थमधिकृत्य उच्यते तदधिकरणम्।[81]

That about which there is elaboration is the subject matter

Illustration -

पृथिव्या लाभे पालने च यावन्त्यर्थशास्त्राणि पूर्वाचार्यैः कृतानि प्रायशस्तानि संहृत्य एकमिदमर्थशास्त्रं कृतम्।

(Kauṭilya Arthaśāstra 1.1)

This Arthaśāstra is made as a compendium of almost all the Arthaśāstras, which, in view of acquisition and maintenance of the earth, have been composed by ancient teachers.

This is the very first statement in the text Kauṭilya Arthaśāstra, which clearly defines the scope and purpose of the work. This is like the title of the work which clarifies the subject matter upfront and also commits the structre in which Kauṭilya will be apporching the work. It is amply evident from even a cursuory study of the work of Kauṭilya that he has profusely referred to the works on Arthaśāstra prior to his period for analysis and discussion.

81 yamarthamadhikṛtya ucyate tadadhikaraṇam|

Example from other texts

विघ्नभूता यदा रोगाः प्रादुर्भूताः शरीरिणाम्। तदा भूतेष्वनुक्रोशं पुरस्कृत्य महर्षयः समेताः पुण्यकर्माणः पार्श्वे हिमवतः शुभे... [82]

(caraka-saṃhitā 1.1.6)

*When diseases began afflicting life, creating impediments to penance (tapas), fasting (upavāsa), study (adhyayana), celibacy (brahmacarya), religious observance (vrata), and the lifespan (**āyuṣ**) of humankind, the holy sages, out of their compassion for all beings, assembled at an auspicious place near the Himalayas.*

The above example for Adhikaraṇa Tantrayukti from Caraka-saṃhitā is given by Cakrapāṇidatta (11th Century CE) in his **Āyurvedadīpikā** commentary on Caraka-saṃhitā.

Notes and Observations

Adhikaraṇa Tantrayuktis reveals several critical aspects. Firstly, it underscores the importance of clearly stating the purpose and approach of a text, necessitating thorough research by the author. Secondly, this clarity in purpose and approach establishes the framework for the treatise's structure, providing a roadmap for the author's exploration of the subject matter. Thirdly, it emphasizes the facilitation of engagement, as without such clarity, neither the author nor the reader can effectively engage with the subject matter, leading to potential confusion or misunderstanding. Additionally, clarity in purpose and approach facilitates meaningful insights and understanding, enriching both the reader's experience and the author's contribution.

82 vighnabhūtā yadā rogāḥ prādurbhūtāḥ śarīriṇām. tadā bhūteṣvanukrośaṃ puraskṛtya maharṣayaḥ sametāḥ puṇyakarmāṇaḥ pārśve himavataḥ śubhe… (carakasaṃ 1.1.6)

Take Aways

For a Researcher:

1. Clarify Purpose and Approach: Articulate the purpose and approach of your research clearly to provide a solid foundation and direction.
2. Establish a Framework: Create a structured framework for your study that outlines the roadmap for exploring the subject matter.

For Evaluators:

1. Evaluate Purpose and Approach: Ensure the thesis articulates its purpose and approach clearly, establishing a strong foundation and direction.
2. Assess Framework Clarity: Verify that the thesis includes a well-defined framework, guiding the exploration of the subject matter.

2. विधानम् Vidhāna

Definition -

शास्त्रस्य प्रकरणानुपूर्वी विधानम्[83]

The sequential arrangement of topics of a treatise.

Illustration -

तस्यायंप्रकरणाधिकरणासमुद्देशः १. विद्यासमुद्देशः २. वृद्धसंयोगः ३. इन्द्रियजयः ४. अमात्योत्पत्तिः ५. अमात्योत्पत्तिः। ६. मन्त्रिपुरोहितोत्पत्तिः। ७. उपधाभिः शचाशौचज्ञानमम। त्यानाम्। ८. गूढपुरुषोत्पत्तिः। ९. गूढपुरुष-प्रणिधिः। १०. स्वविषये कृत्याकृत्यपक्षरक्षणम्। ११. परविषये कृत्याकृत्यपक्षोपग्रहः। १२. मन्त्राधिकारः। १३. दूतप्रणिधिः। १४. राजपुत्ररक्षणम्। १५. अवरुद्धवृत्तम्। १६. अवरुद्धेच वृत्तिः। १७. राजप्रणिधिः। १८. निशान्तप्रणिधिः। १९. आत्मरक्षितकम्। इति विनयाधिकारिकंप्रथमाधिकरणम् ॥[84]

---

83 śāstrasya prakaraṇānupūrvī vidhānam

84 tasyāyaṃ prakaraṇādhikaraṇāsamuddeśaḥ 1. vidyāsamuddeśaḥ 2. vṛddhasaṃyogaḥ 3. indriyajayaḥ 4. amātyotpattiḥ 4. amātyotpattiḥ. 5. mantripurohitotpattiḥ. 6. upadhābhiḥ śau- 'cāśaucajñānamama. tyānām. 7. gūḍhapuruṣotpattiḥ. 8. gūḍhapuruṣapra- ṇidhiḥ. 9. svaviṣaye kṛtyākṛtyapakṣarakṣaṇam. 10. paraviṣaye kṛtyākṛtyapakṣopagrahaḥ. 11. mantrādhikāraḥ. 12. dūtapraṇidhiḥ. 13. rājaputrarakṣaṇam. 14. avaruddhavṛttam. 15. avaruddhe ca vṛttiḥ. 16. rājapraṇidhiḥ. 17. niśāntapraṇidhiḥ. 18. ātmarakṣitakam. iti vinayādhikārikaṃ prathamādhikaraṇam..

(Of that (treatise), this is an enumeration of Sections and Books) – 1. The end of Sciences; 2. association with the aged; 3. restraint of the organs of sense; 4. the creation of ministers; 5. the creation of councillors and priests; 6. ascertaining by temptations purity or impurity in the character of ministers; 7. the institution of spies. (8. Duties of a spy), 9.Protection of parties for or against one's own cause in one's own state; 10.winning over the factions for or against an enemy's cause in an enemy's state; 11.the business of council meeting; 12.the mission of envoys; 13.protection of princes; 14. the conduct of a prince kept under restraint; 15. treatment of a prince kept under restraint; 16. the duties of a king; 17.duty towards the harem; 18.personal safety – (these constitute the first book concerning the topic of training)

As is evident, the table of contents of the first *Adhikaraṇa* has been provided by Kauṭilya. It is to be noted that, for want of space, not all the subtopics discussed in the remaining 14 Adhikaraṇas have been included. Kauṭilya was meticulous in mentioning all the subtopics of each Adhikaraṇa.

Example from other texts

Consider a similar application of the Yuktis in **Kāvyamīmāṃsā** of **Rājaśekhara -**

तस्या अयं प्रकरणाधिकरणसमुद्देशः। शास्त्रसङ्ग्रहः शास्त्रनिर्देशः, काव्यपुरुषोत्पत्तिः, पदवाक्यविवेकः, पाठप्रतिष्ठा, अर्थानुशासनं, वाक्यविधयः, कविविशेषः, कविचर्या, राजचर्या, काकुप्रकाराः, शब्दार्थहरणोपायाः, कविसमयः, देशकालविभागः, भुवनकोश, इति कविरहस्यं प्रथममधिकरणमित्यादि।[85]

85 tasyā ayaṃ prakaraṇādhikaraṇasamuddeśaḥ. śāstrasaṅgrahaḥ śāstranirdeśaḥ, kāvyapuruṣotpattiḥ, padavākyavivekaḥ, pāṭhapratiṣṭhā, arthānuśāsanaṃ, vākyavidhayaḥ, kaviviśeṣaḥ, kavicaryā, rājacaryā, kākuprakārāḥ, śabdārthaharaṇopāyāḥ, kavisamayaḥ, deśakālavibhāgaḥ, bhuvanakośa, iti kavirahasyaṃ prathamamadhikaraṇamityādi. (This appears right in the beginning of the text.)

(Of that (treatise), this is an enumeration of Sections and Books) – Essence of shastra, Instruction of the shastra, Origin of the Kavya Puruṣa, Analysis of Padavākya, Text Establishment, Discipline of Meaning, Sentence Methods, Special Poet, Poetry, Royalty, Types of Kaku, Ways of Harnessing Semantics, poetic convention, Division of Country and Time, World Encyclopedia – thus the first chapter

Notes and Observations

Vidhāna serves as a vital component of structuring a thesis, complementing the basic content and approach discussed in the initial Yuktis (Adhikaraṇa).

Take Aways

For a Researcher:

Ensure that the subject matter is systematically arranged under various topics and present this sequence at the outset of the text. Adopt a methodical, topic-wise approach to ensure coherence and logical progression in the presentation of ideas..

For Evaluators:

Utilize Table of Contents as a tool to gain a clear overview of the thesis's structure, guiding you through its organization and flow. Assess the coherence, completeness, and depth of the research with its assistance offering insight into the author's scholarly rigor

3. उद्देशः Uddeśa

Definition -

समसवाक्यम् उद्देशः।[86]

Brief statement of the content of a section and its limbs – for due elaboration.

Illustration -

विद्याविनयहेतुरिन्द्रियजयः।[87]

(Kauṭilya Arthaśāstra 1.6)

The conquest over the senses is the cause for learning and humility.

This is a brief statement about conquest of the senses. This creates an interest to know more about what the conquest of the senses means and how it leads to learning and humility. Such a brief statement that creates and expectation for elaboration is Uddeśa.

Example from other texts

This is a popular Yuktis applied by many texts of Indian knowledge systems cutting across disciplines. Some examples are as follows -

86 samasavākyam uddeśaḥ.

87 vidyāvinayaheturindriyajayaḥ. (arthaśā 1.6)

वायुः पित्तं कफश्चेति त्रयो दोषाः समासतः।[88]

(aṣṭāṅga-hṛdaya-sūtra 1.6)

In brief, Vata, Pitta and Kapha are the three Doshas.

द्रव्यगुणकर्मसामान्यविशेष-समवायाभावाः सप्तपदार्थाः[89]

(tarka-saṃgrahaḥ)

Dravya, Guṇa, Karma, Sāmānya, Viśeṣa, Samavāya, and Abhāva are the seven Padārthas.

प्रमाणविपर्ययविकल्पनिद्रास्मृतयः[90]

(yoga-sūtra 1.6)

Pramāṇa, Viparyaya, Vikalpa, Nidrā and smṛti (are the five Vṛttis)

It is noteworthy that, in each of the quoted examples above, the treatises present a list of the constituents of a particular set. This naturally sparks curiosity in the reader to learn more about the set as a whole and each of its constituents.

Notes and Observations

Uddeśa Yuktis contributes to the structuring of treatises by focusing on the discussion of specific topics. It emphasizes the importance of presenting a concise statement at the outset of each topic, as demonstrated in texts like the Arthaśāstra. This approach helps readers easily recall the essence of each chapter's discussion. Even if the entire content cannot be remembered, recalling the Uddeśa sentences simplifies the process. It is important to note that Uddeśa Yuktis is complemented by a subsequent Yuktis (Nirdeśa). Brief statements

88 vāyuḥ pittaṃ kaphaśceti trayo doṣāḥ samāsataḥ. (ahṛsū 1.6)

89 dravyaguṇakarmasāmānyaviśeṣa-samavāyābhāvāḥ saptapadārthāḥ (tarkasaṃgrahaḥ)

90 pramāṇaviparyayavikalpanidrāsmṛtayaḥ (yo.sū 1.6)

without proper elaboration can lead to disconnection and a lack of coherence in the text.

Take Aways

For Researchers:

Meticulously plan the commencement of each section of a thesis. It is not enough to provide only a macro structure; attention to detail in every section is imperative for creating a concise and enduring treatise.

For Evaluators:

Pay attention on how the content of a section is commited in the commencement of a section.

4. निर्देशः Nirdeśa

Definition -

व्यासवाक्यं निर्देशः।[91]

A detailed statement is explanation [92]

Illustration -

कर्णात्वगक्षिजिह्वाघ्राणेन्द्रियाणां शब्दस्पर्शरूपरसगन्धेषु
अप्रतिपत्तिरिन्द्रियजयः [93]

(Kauṭilya Arthaśāstra 1.6)

Absence of discrepancy[94] *in the perception of sound, touch, colour, flavour, and scent by means of the ear, the skin, the eyes, the tongue, and the nose, is what is meant by restraint of the organs of sense*

In the example of Uddeśa Indriya-jaya (conquest of Senses) was mentioned. Here the concept of Indriya jaya is systematically elaborated by sequentially mentioning the list of the senses of sound, touch … and their respective objects and the absence of improper indulgence is mentioned as its conquest.

---

91 vyāsavākyaṃ nirdeśaḥ

92 The above shamasttry translation is from RP Kangle (RP Kangle, 2010, pg.512)

93 karṇātvagakṣijihvāghrāṇendriyāṇāṃ śabdasparśarūparasagandheṣu apratipattirindriyajayaḥ (arthaśā 1.6)

94 improper indulgence (RP Kangle, 2010, pg.512)

Example from other texts

तत्र रूक्षो लघुः शीतः खरः सूक्ष्मश्चलोऽनिलः।
पित्तं सस्नेहतीक्ष्णोष्णं लघु विस्त्रं सरं द्रवम् ॥11॥
स्निग्धः शीतो गुरुर्मन्दः श्लक्ष्णो मृत्स्नः स्थिरः कफः।[95]

(aṣṭāṅga-hṛdaya-sūtra 1.11)

Rūkṣa (dryness), laghu (lightness, weightlessness), śīta (coldness), khara (roughness), sūkṣma (minuteness), and cala (movement, unsteadiness) are the qualities of Anila (Vāta). Sasneha (slight unctuousness), tīkṣṇa (penetrating), uṣṇa (hot, heat-producing), laghu (lightness), visra *(bad smell),* sara *(causing movement), and drava (liquidity) are the qualities of Pitta. Snigdha (unctuousness), śīta (cold, producing coldness), guru (heaviness), manda (sluggish, slow), ślakṣṇa (smoothness, slipperiness), mṛtsna (shining), and sthira (firm, static) are the qualities of Kapha.*

तत्र द्रव्याणि पृथिव्यप्तेजोवाय्वाकाशकालदिगात्ममनांसि नवैव ॥ ३ ॥
रूप-रस- गन्ध-स्पर्श संख्या- परिमाण -पृथक्त्व-संयोग-विभाग- परत्वा-ऽपरत्व-गुरुत्व- द्रवत्व-स्नेह-शब्द-बुद्धि-सुख -दुःखेच्छा द्वेष-प्रयत्न-धर्माधर्म-संस्काराः चतुर्विंशतिर्गुणाः ४ ॥[96]

Of the seven categories the siubstances are only nine – viz earth, water, light, air, ether, time, space and soul. 3
Colour, taste, odour, touch, number, magnitude, separateness, conjunction, disjunction, remoteness, proximity, weight, fluidity, viscidity, sound, intellect, pleasure, pain, desire, aversion, volition, merit, demerit and tendency are the twenty-four qualities. 4

Yogasūtras (1.7-11)

---

95 tatra rūkṣo laghuḥ śītaḥ kharaḥ sūkṣmaścalo'nilaḥ. pittaṃ sasnehatīkṣṇoṣṇaṃ laghu vistraṃ saraṃ dravam..11.. snigdhaḥ śīto gururmandaḥ ślakṣṇo mṛtsnaḥ sthiraḥ kaphaḥ.(ahṛsū 1.11)

96 tatra dravyāṇi pṛthivyaptejovāyvākāśakāladigātmamanāṃsi navaiva.. 3.. rūpa-rasa- gandha-sparśa saṃkhyā- parimāṇa - pṛthaktva-saṃyoga-vibhāga-paratvā-'paratva-gurutva- dravatva-sneha-śabda- buddhi-sukha - duḥkhecchā dveṣa- prayatna-dharmādharma-saṃskārāḥ caturviṃśatirguṇāḥ.. 4..

प्रत्यक्षानुमानागमाः प्रमाणानि ॥
विपर्ययो मिथ्याज्ञानमतद्रूपप्रतिष्ठम् ॥
शब्दज्ञानानुपाती वस्तुशून्यो विकल्पः॥
अभावप्रययालम्बना वृत्तिर्निद्रा ॥
अनुभूतविषयासंप्रमोषः स्मृतिः ॥ ११[97]

(These are) right knowledge (pramāṇa), indiscrimination (viparyaya), verbal delusion (vikalpa), sleep (nidrā), and memory (smṛti). 1.7 Indiscrimination is false knowledge not established in real nature. 1.8 Verbal delusion follows from words having no (corresponding) reality. 1.9 Sleep is a Vṛtti which embraces the feeling of voidness. 1.10 Memory is when the (Vṛttis of) perceived subjects do not slip away (and through impressions come back to consciousness). 1.11

Notes and Observations

This analysis of various texts demonstrates the importance of systematically elaborating (Nirdeśa Yukti) upon brief statements or enumerated components, showcasing how this approach is employed in different treatises such as the Arthaśāstra, Caraka-saṃhitā, Tarkasaṅgraha, and Yogasūtra. Such understanding can inform the structuring of a thesis by emphasizing the necessity of coherence between initial statements and subsequent elaborations, contributing to a clear and organized presentation of arguments or findings. The transition from concise statements to systematic elaborations facilitates a deeper understanding and clarity for the reader. The structured approach enhances reader engagement and comprehension by guiding them through a logical progression of ideas.

97 pramāṇaviparyayavikalpanidrāsmṛtaya ॥ 1.6 ॥, pratyakṣānumānāgamāḥ pramāṇāni ॥ 1.7 ॥
viparyayo mithyājñānamatadrūpapratiṣṭham ॥ 1.8 ॥, śabdajñānānupātī vastuśūnyo vikalpaḥ ॥ 1.9 ॥
abhāvaprayayālambanā vṛttirnidrā ॥ 1.10 ॥, anubhūtaviṣayāsaṁpramoṣaḥ smṛtiḥ ॥ 1.11 ॥

Take Aways

For a Researcher:

Ensure coherence between the initial statements and subsequent elaborations in a chapter to ensure structural integrity and effectiveness.

For Evaluators:

Assess how well the initial statements align with their elaborations towards breaking down complex ideas concisely and logically.

5. पूर्वपक्षः Pūrvapakṣa

Definition -

प्रतिषेद्धव्यं वाक्यं पूर्वपक्षः।[98]

The view that has to be rejected is primafacie view

Illustration -

स्वाम्यमात्यव्यसनयोः अमात्यव्यसनं गरीयः- भरद्वाजः[99]

(Kauṭilya Arthaśāstra 8.1)

Of the two evils, the distress of the king and that of his minister, the latter is worse – says Bharadvāja

It is to be noted that this view is later refuted by Kauṭilya, who states that the calamities of the king are greater. It is also important to note that a prima facie view should also have justification. Kauṭilya quotes the following justification given by *Bharadvāja* for stating that the calamity of the minister is greater:

नेति भारद्वाजः। स्वाम्यमात्यव्यसनयोरमात्यव्यसनं गरीय
इति। मन्त्रो मन्त्रफलावाप्तिः कर्मानुष्ठानमायव्ययकर्म दण्डप्रणयनम-
मित्राटवीप्रतिषेधो राज्यरक्षणं व्यसनप्रतीकारः कुमाररक्षणमभिषेकच
कुमाराणामायत्तममात्येषु। तेषाम् अभावे तदभावः, छिन्नपक्षस्येवं

98 pratiṣeddhavyaṃ vākyaṃ pūrvapakṣaḥ

99 svāmyamātyavyasanayoḥ amātyavyasanaṃ garīyaḥ. - bharadvājaḥ (arthaśā 8.1)

राज्ञश्रेष्टानाशः। व्यसनेषु चासन्नाः परोपजापाः। वैगुण्ये च प्राण- बाधः प्राणान्तिकचरत्वाद् राज्ञ इति [100]

(Kauṭilya Arthaśāstra 8.1)

"No" Says Bharadvāja. Amidst distress to King and Minister, Ministerial distress is more serious; deliberations in council, the attainment of results as anticipated while deliberating in council, the accomplishment of works, the business of revenue-collection and its expenditure, recruiting the army, the driving out of the enemy and of wild tribes, the protection of the kingdom, taking remedial measures against calamities, the protection of the heir-apparent, and the installation of princes constitute the duties of ministers. In the absence of ministers; the above works are ill-done; and like a bird, deprived of its feathers, the king loses his active capacity. In such calamities, the intrigues of the enemy find a ready scope. In ministerial distress, the king's life itself comes into danger, for a minister is the mainstay of the security of the king's life" (Kauṭilya Arthaśāstra 7.1)

Example from other texts

न मत्स्यान् पयसा सह अभ्यवहरेत् - आत्रेयवचनम्।
(पूर्वपक्ष:) सर्वानेव मत्स्यान् पयसा अभ्यवहरेत् अन्यत्र चिलिचिमात् इति भद्रकाप्यवचनम्

(Caraka-saṃhitā 1.26. 82,83)

100 neti bhāradvājaḥ. svāmyamātyavyasanayoramātyavyasanaṃ garīya iti. mantro mantraphalāvāptiḥ karmānuṣṭhānamāyavyayakarma daṇḍapraṇayanamamitrāṭavīpratiṣedho rājyarakṣaṇaṃ vyasanapratīkāraḥ kumārarakṣaṇamabhiṣekaca kumārāṇāmāyattamamātyeṣu. teṣām abhāve tadabhāvaḥ, chinnapakṣasyevaṃ rājñaśreṣṭānāśaḥ. vyasaneṣu cāsannāḥ paropajāpāḥ. vaiguṇye ca prāṇa- bādhaḥ prāṇāntikacaratvād rājña iti

One should not consume fish with milk[101]

(Prima facie view) Excepting Cilicima fish, one can consume all kinds of fishes with milk[102]

Notes and Observations

In research, addressing potential objections is vital for robust scholarship. Anticipating and resolving objections demonstrates thoroughness, strengthens arguments, and enhances credibility. It fosters a nuanced understanding of the topic and ensures the work contributes meaningfully to the academic discourse, promoting rigorous inquiry and intellectual integrity. Most texts of Indian Knowledge Systems, especially the commentary literature, are rich in raising systematic and graded potential objections and resolving them.

Take Aways

For Researchers:

1. Ensure the validity and credibility of theories by proactively addressing potential objections, presenting comprehensive presentations of objections and prima facie views along with resolutions to withstand scrutiny and establish a solid theoretical foundation.

---

101 Context: *Ātreya* says, "...I will mention the incompatible (*vairodhika*) food which is mostly used, such as, one should not take fish with milk. Both of them have *madhura* (*rasa*). *Madhura vipāka*, *mahabhīṣyandi* (great obstructor of the channels), because milk is *śīta* and fish is *uṣṇa*, which is *viruddhavyīrya* (antagonistic in terms of *vīrya*). Due to conflicting *vīryas*, it vitiates blood and, due to being *mahabhīṣyandi*, creates obstruction in the channels." [82]

102 Context: *Bhadrakāpya's* prima facie view: Having heard the statement of *Ātreya*, *Bhadrakāpya* said to *Agniveśa*, "One may take all types of fish along with milk, except for one—*chilchimā*. That scaly, red-eyed fish, with all-around red stripes and shaped like *rohita*, often moves on land. If one takes it along with milk, he undoubtedly becomes a victim of one of the disorders of *rakta* (blood), *vibandha* (constipation), or even death." This view is later refuted.

2. Avoid careless or incomplete representations, ensuring thorough presentation with justifications to strengthen subsequent discussions and resolutions within the thesis.

For Evaluators:

1. Scrutinize how potential objections to the proposed theory are brought forth confidently.
2. Look for comprehensive presentations of objections, prima facie views, to establish a robust theoretical foundation.

6. उत्तरपक्षः/निर्णयः/प्रत्युत्सारः uttarapakṣaḥ / nirṇayaḥ / pratyutsāraḥ

Definition -

तस्य निर्णयवाक्यम् उत्तरपक्षः[103]

Settled opinion is rejoinder

Illustration -

नेति कौटल्यः। मन्त्रिपुरोहितादिभृत्यवर्गमध्यक्षप्रचारं पुरुष-द्रव्यप्रकृतिव्यसनप्रतीकारमेधनं च राजैव करोति। व्यसनिषु वामात्येष्वन्यानव्यसनिनः करोति। पूज्यपूजने दूष्यावग्रहे च नित्ययुक्तस्तिष्ठति। स्वामी च सम्पन्नः स्वसम्पद्भिः प्रकृतीः सम्पादयति। स्वयं यच्छीलस्तच्छीलाः प्रकृतयो भवन्ति, उत्थाने प्रमादे च तदाय- चत्वात्। तत्कूटस्थानीयो हि स्वामीति। (अर्थशा ८.१)[104]

No, says Kauṭilya, it is verily the king who attends to the business of appointing ministers, priests, and other servants, including the

---

103 tasya nirṇayavākyam uttarapakṣaḥ

104 neti kauṭalyaḥ. mantripurohitādibhṛtyavargamadhyakṣapracāraṃ puruṣa-dravyaprakṛtivyasanapratīkāramedhanaṃ ca rājaiva karoti. vyasaniṣu vāmātyeṣvanyānavyasaninaḥ karoti. pūjyapūjane dūṣyāvagrahe ca nityayuktastiṣṭhati. svāmī ca sampannaḥ svasampadbhiḥ prakṛtīḥ sampādayati. svayaṃ yacchīlastacchīlāḥ prakṛtayo bhavanti, utthāne pramāde ca tadāya- catvāt. tatkūṭasthānīyo hi svāmīti.

superintendents of several departments, the application of remedies against the troubles of his people, and of his kingdom, and the adoption of progressive measures; when his ministers fall into troubles, he employs others; he is ever ready to bestow rewards on the worthy and inflict punishments on the wicked; when the king is well off, by his welfare and prosperity, he pleases the people; of what kind the king's character is, of the same kind will be the character of his people; for their progress or downfall, the people depend upon the king; the king is, as it were, the aggregate of the people.

This illustration is a continuation from the illustration of the previous Yukti. Bharadvāja was of the view that the calamity/distress of the minister is greater than that of the distresss of the king even. That was the primafacie view and that is refuted and final view is established by the author through the self-evident example given above, which illustrates that Uttarapakṣa Yukti.

Example from other texts

नेति भगवानात्रेयः- सर्वानेव मत्स्यान्न पयसा सहाभ्यवहरेद्विशेषतस्तु
चिलिचिमं, स हि महाभिष्यन्दित्वात् स्थूललक्षणतरानेतान्
व्याधीनुपजनयत्यामविषमुदीरयति च।[105]

(caraka-saṃhitā 1.26.82-83)

"No", said Lord Ātreya. "One should not take any fish along with milk particularly chilchimā because it being a great obstructor of channels produces these disorders with gross symptoms and also excites āmaviṣa.[106]

---

105 neti bhagavānātreyaḥ- sarvāneva matsyānna payasā sahābhyavaharedviśeṣatastu cilicimaṃ, sa hi mahābhiṣyanditvāt sthūlalakṣaṇatarānetān vyādhīnupajanayatyāmaviṣamudīrayati ca| (carakasaṃ 1.26. 82-83)

106 …he undoubtedly becomes victim of one of the disorders of rakta (blood) or vibandha (constipation) or death… CS 1.26.82

Note: This is also the continuation of the illustration from the Caraka-saṃhitā example given for the previous Yukti. Innumerable examples can be culled from the vast Saṃskṛta Literature to illustrate this and the previous Yukti. It is the firm foundation upon which the time-tested superstructure of knowledge system has sustained itself through ages.

Notes and Observations

Structurally, Pūrvapakṣa and Uttarapakṣa Yuktis play crucial roles in constructing a thesis. The expansion of a brief statement, as facilitated by Uddeśa and Nirdeśa Tantra Yukti, includes addressing objections and their refutations. These two Yuktis —Pūrvapakṣa and Uttarapakṣa—should be nested under the Nirdeśa Tantrayuktis. Objections to any presented view can be systematically stacked and discussed, either based on simplicity to complexity or vice versa, making the exposition comprehensive and convincing.

Take Aways

For Researchers:

1. Go beyond simple rejection; rigorously and in justified manner refute objections to strengthen research integrity.
2. Showcase your capacity to logically counter opposing views, reinforcing your research's solidity and demonstrating your scholarly acumen.

For Evaluators:

Evaluate how effectively and comprehensively the objections and potential objections are countered to gauge both the research's robustness and the researcher's competency.

7. अतिक्रातावेक्षणम् atikrāntāvekṣaṇa

Definition -

पुरस्तादेवं विहितमित्यतिक्रान्तावेक्षणम्[107]

Stating that it has been already spoken of earlier

Illustration -

"अमात्य-सम्पदुक्ता पुरस्तात्" इति

(Kauṭilya Arthaśāstra 6.1)

The Qualifications of a minister has been stated earlier.

The above sentence appears in the chapter 6.1 on the elements of Sovernignity which includes the king, the minister, the country, the fort, the treasury, the army and the friend are the elements of sovereignty. Each of the element (king, minister, country…) is discussed in detail. When it comes to the elaboration minister the above statement is made (qualities of the minister has been stated earlier).

107 purastādevaṃ vihitamityatikrāntāvekṣaṇam

It is to be noted that in chapter 1.9 (on the section of creation of councillors and ministers)[108] itself the qualifications of the minister has been elaborated. Hence this is not repeated in a later occasion (6.1)

Example from other texts

त्रयोदशविधः स्वेदः स्वेदाध्याये निदर्शितः।
मात्राकालविदा युक्तः स च शीतज्वरापहः॥[109]

(caraka-saṃhitā – 6.3.238)

Thirteen varieties of sveda procedures have been described in the Svedādhyāya of Sūtra Sthāna. A physician who is well-versed with the proper duration of sveda as suitable to the season and person should administer them for the treatment of śīta jvara.

The above statement appears in the cikitsā-sthāna 6.3.238 which is about treating fevers. Svedana is prescribed as a method of treating śīta jvara. With regard to the process of sudation it is clarified that it has already been elaborated in the 14th Section of Sūtrasthana (1.14). This is Atikrāntāvekṣaṇam.

Notes and Observations

This and the next Yuktis are crucial structural devices in a text. They streamline the presentation by avoiding redundant explanations of concepts already elaborated elsewhere. Readers gain insights into different dimensions of the topic by observing its relevance in various contexts. Referencing related discussions helps readers understand additional aspects of the topic under discussion

---

108 Native, born of high family, influential, well trained in arts, possessed of foresight, wise, of strong memory, bold, eloquent, skillful, intelligent, possessed of enthusiasm, dignity, and endurance, pure in character, affable, firm in loyal devotion, endowed with excellent conduct, strength, health and bravery, free from procrastination and ficklemindedness, affectionate, and free from such qualities as excite hatred and enmity--these are the qualifications of a ministerial officer (amátyasampat). (1.9)

109 trayodaśavidhaḥ svedaḥ svedādhyāye nidarśitaḥ|mātrākālavidā yuktaḥ sa ca śītajvarāpahaḥ||268||

Take Aways

For Researchers:

Use the commonsense approach of referencing previously explained concepts to reduce text volume. Demonstrate complete awareness of your own work and ensure a tight and compact presentation.

For Evaluators:

Note the judicious use of this structural device of referencing to a past statement that indicates author's ability to maintain coherence and avoid redundancy contributing to the text's tightness.

8. अनागतावेक्षणम् Anāgatāvekṣaṇa

Definition -

पश्चादेवं विहितमित्यनागतावेक्षणम्[110]

Drawing attention to a later chapter is reference to a subsequent portion

Illustration -

तुलाप्रतिमानं पौतवाध्यक्षे वक्ष्यामः[111]

(Kauṭilya Arthaśāstra 2.13)

We shall explain balance and weights in the chapter 'The Superintendent of Weights and Measures

In Adhikaraṇa 2 Chapter 13 the "Superintendent of Gold in the Goldsmith's office" is being discussed where various qualities of Gold are discussed. In that context – Gold has to be measured. But those measuring details are elaborated in a later Adhikaraṇa 2 Chapter19 which is on 'The Superintendent of Weights and Measures"

110 paścādevaṃ vihitamityanāgatāvekṣaṇam
111 tulāpratimānaṃ pautavādhyakakṣe vakṣyāmaḥ

Example from other texts

श्लोकस्थाने ब्रूयात् चिकित्सितेषु वक्ष्यामीति...[112]

(suśruta-saṃhitā uttara-tantra 65.30)

For example—it is stated in the sūtra-sthana 'it will be dealt with in the Cikitsāsthāna'.

The following is the elaboration of the Yuktis -

एतदष्टविधं (शस्त्र)कर्म समासेन प्रकीर्तितम्
चिकित्सितेषु (4) कार्त्स्न्येन विस्तरस्तस्य वक्ष्यते

(suśruta-saṃhitā – 1.25.29)[113]

Thus the eight types of surgical procedures[114] have been described in brief. The entire details of this will be stated in the Cikitsāsthāna.

It is to be noted that Sūtra-sthāna is the first book and the Cikitsā-sthāna comes as the fourth book. A later elaboration has been briefly stated here. Hence this is an example for Anāgatāvekṣaṇa.

Notes and Observations

The implications of this Yuktis is the same as that of the previous Yukti.

---

112 ślokasthāne brūyāt cikitsiteṣu vakṣyāmīti… (suśrutasāṃhitā uttaratantram 65. 30)

113 etadaṣṭavidhaṃ (śastra) karma samāsena prakīrtitam cikitsiteṣu (4) kārtsnyena vistarastasya vakṣyate (suśrutasaṃhitā – 1.25.29)

114 छेद्य-भेद्य-लेख्य-वेध्य-एष्य-आहार्य-विस्राव्य-सीव्य-भेदा chedya-bhedya-lekhya-vedhya-eṣya-āhārya-visrāvya-sīvya-bhedā Chedya (excision), Lekhya (scarification), Vedhya (puncturing), eṣya (exploration), āhrya (extraction), viśraya (evacuation), and sīvya (suturing)

9. अतिदेशः Atideśa

Definition -

उक्तेन साधनम् अतिदेशः[115]

When a rule dwelt upon in connection with a question is said to apply to another question also, it is termed application

Illustration -

दत्तस्यादानमृणादानवद् व्याख्येयम्[116]

(Kauṭilya Arthaśāstra 11.3)

What is said of a debt not repaid holds good with failure to make good a promised gift.

We can see here that – measures to be taken if a person defaults to return the loan taken has been stated in Chapter 11 of Book 3. Now when the discussion of not honouring the commitment of gifts promised arises later in chapter 16 of the same book, it is said that the same measures are to be taken here also, as was stated in connection to non-returing of a loan. This is Yuktis Atideśa.

115 uktena sādhanam atideśaḥ

116 dattasyādānamṛṇādānavad vyākhyeyam

Example from other texts

एष एव विधिः कार्यः शिशिरे समुदाहृतः[117]

(suśruta-saṃhitā uttara-tantra 64.31)

The same rule has to be extended that has been stated in connection with the Śiśira (winter) season

To explain this – This sentence appears in the context of ṛtucaryā– seasonally appropriate lifestyle practices. After stating the seasonally appropriate practices for Hemanta season (early winter), it is stated that the same rules are to be followed for the Śiśira Season (winter season). It is to be noted that Hemanta and Śiśira are both cold seasons that come one after the other. Hence the one that has been stated for Śiśira has to be taken for Hemanta also.

Notes and Observations

The Yuktis Atikrāntāvekṣaṇa and Anāgatāvekṣaṇa aid in referencing descriptions earlier or later in the text, while the Yuktis Atideśa, applies rules from earlier contexts to later ones. Illustrations from Arthaśāstra and Suśruta-saṃhitā vividly demonstrate this concept. The incorporation of Atideśa within a thesis framework enhances the organization and coherence of the text by facilitating the referencing of descriptions and the application of rules across different sections.

Take Aways

For Researchers:

Utilize a rule created appropriately and optimally across different relevant contexts of the thesis

For Evaluators:

Note the application of this Yuktis in thesis which is a mark of good research that avoids redundant rule creation.

---

117 eṣa eva vidhiḥ kāryaḥ śiśire samudāhṛtaḥ

10. प्रदेशः Pradeśa

Definition -

वक्तव्येन साधनं प्रदेशः।[118]

Establishing a fact by what is to be treated later is Place of reference

Illustration -

सामदानभेददण्डैः वा यथापत्सु व्याख्यास्यामः।[119]

(Kauṭilya Arthaśāstra 7.14)

By making use of such strategic means as conciliation, bribery, dissension, and coercion, as we shall explain in connection with calamities.

The chapter in which the above quote appears (7.14) discusses regaining lost power from the conquerer. Each of the four means such as conciliation or bribery or dissension or coercion can be used to achived the desired result. Or all the four can be used. This method shall be explained in the 5th Chapter of the 9th book which is designated as section on calamities (āpatprakaraṇam).[120]

---

118 vaktavyena sādhanaṃ pradeśaḥ.

119 sāmadānabhedadaṇḍaiḥ vā yathāpatsu vyākhyāsyāmaḥ. -arthaśā 7.14

120 As the definition of the Yuktis differes in other texts, illustration is also different. Hence example from other texts have not been given.

Notes and Observations

The implications of the Yuktis for researchers and evaluators are same as that of the previous Yukti.

11. प्रसङ्गः Prasaṅga

Definition -

प्रकरणान्तरेण समानः अर्थः[121]

When the nature of procedure to be specified in connection with a thing is said to be equal to what has already been specified in connection with another, it is termed reference to similar procedure.

Illustration -

कर्षको वृत्तिक्षीणः प्रज्ञाशौचयुक्तः गृहपतिकव्यञ्जनः
कृषिकर्मप्रदिष्टायाम् भूमौ इति समानं पूर्वेण[122]

(Kauṭilya Arthaśāstra 1.11)

A cultivator, fallen from his profession, but possessed of foresight and pure character is termed a householder spy. This spy shall carry on the cultivation of lands allotted to him for the purpose, and maintain cultivators, etc. - as before.

The above example is from the section on appointment of Spies Kauṭilya Arthaśāstra Adhikaraṇa 1 chapter 11. The quotation above describes the recruiting and defining the function of Gṛhapatika spy (householder spy). It can be noted that after giving few descrptions – it has been

121 prakaraṇāntareṇa samānaḥ arthaḥ

122 karṣako vṛttikṣīṇaḥ prajñāśaucayuktaḥ gṛhapatikavyañjanaḥ kṛṣikarmapradiṣṭāyām bhūmau iti samānaṃ pūrveṇa (udāsthitena).(arthaśā 1.11)

stated "it is same as above". The paragraph that precedes the descrption on Gṛhapatika spy is description of udāsthita Spy (spy in the form of a reculse). The descrption is as follows -

One who is initiated in asceticism and is possessed of foresight and pure character is a recluse. This spy, provided with much money and many disciples, shall carry on agriculture, cattle-rearing, and trade (vártakarma) on the lands allotted to him for the purpose. Out of the produce and profits thus acquired, he shall provide all ascetics with subsistence, clothing and lodging, and send on espionage such among those under his protection as are desirous to earn a livelihood (vrittikáma), ordering each of them to detect a particular kind of crime committed in connection with the king's wealth and to report of it when they come to receive their subsistence and wages. All the ascetics (under the recluse) shall severally send their followers on similar errands. [123]

It is to be understood that all the underlined section are same for the Gṛhapatika Spy that follows this paragraph. This is the application of Tantrayuktis Prasaṅga which avoids repeating aspects that are same with that of the previous point under discussion.[124]

Example from other texts

The Yuktis Prasaṅga is found used repeatedly in Saṃskṛta literature. In many texts the expression "शेषं पूर्ववत्" or merely पूर्ववत् (rest as earlier) could be found which is the indication of the utilization of the Yukti. References to the occurrence of the above expression in texts

123 प्रव्रज्याप्रत्यवसितः प्रज्ञाशौचयुक्त उदास्थितः। स वार्त्ताकर्मप्रदिष्टायां भूमौ प्रभूतहिरण्यान्तेवासी कर्म कारयेत्। कर्मफलाच्च सर्वप्रव्रजितानां ग्रासाच्छादनावसथान् प्रतिविदध्यात्। वृत्तिकामांश्चोपजपेत्, एतेनैव वेषेण राजार्थश्चरितव्यो भक्तवेतनकाले चोपस्थातव्य- मिति। सर्वप्रव्रजिताश्च स्वं स्वं वर्गमुपजपेयुः। pravrajyāpratyavasitaḥ prajñāśaucayukta udāsthita. sa vārttākarmapradiṣṭāyāṃ bhūmau prabhūtahiraṇyāntevāsī karma kārayet.karmaphalāccasarvapravrajitānāṃgrāsācchādanāvasathānpratividadhyāt. vṛttikāmāṃścopajapet, etenaiva veṣeṇa rājārthaścaritavyo bhaktavetanakāle copasthātavya- miti. sarvapravrajitāśca svaṃ svaṃ vargamupajapeyuḥ.

124 Definition and illustration of the Yuktis is presented differently in Caraka and suśruta saṃhitā hence example from other texts are not given.

cutting across disciplines is given – ऋग्वेदसायणभाष्यम् (1.140.1), समराङ्गणसूत्रधारः (60.104) अग्निपुराणम् (117.34), हठयोगप्रदीपिका (2.51)[125]

Notes and Observation

In contrast to the preceding four Yuktis, Atikrāntāvekṣaṇa, Anāgatāvekṣaṇa, Atideśa, and Pradeśa, which focus on reusing content from earlier or later sections, Prasaṅga Yuktis pertains to content within the same section, emphasizing the avoidance of repetition. This technique succinctly conveys the essence of the Yukti, promoting a compact and cohesive structure within the text while ensuring brevity.

Take Aways

For Researchers:

Eliminate redundant passages, repetitive descrptions, demonstrating diligence and attention to detail.

For Evaluators:

Look for the researcher's commitment to avoiding verbosity and towards maintaining clarity in the presentation of ideas.

---

125 ṛgvedasāyaṇabhāṣyam (1.140.1), samarāṅgaṇasūtradhāraḥ (adhyāya 60 ślokaḥ 104) agnipurāṇam haṭhayogapradīpikā 2.51 (adhyāyaḥ 117 ślokaḥ 34)

12. विपर्ययः Viparyaya

Definition -

प्रतिलोमेन साधनं विपर्ययः[126]

The inference of a reverse statement from a positive statement is termed contrariety

Illustration -

परस्य वाचि वक्त्रे दृष्ट्यां च प्रसादं वाक्यपूजनमिष्टपरिप्रश्नं गुणकथासङ्गमासन्नमासनं सत्कारमिष्टेषु स्मरणं विश्वासगमनं च लक्षयेत् तुष्टस्य, विपरीतमतुष्टस्य[127]

(Kauṭilya Arthaśāstra 1.16)

Brightness in the tone, face, and eyes of the enemy; respectful reception of the mission; enquiry about the health of friends; taking part in the narration of virtues; giving a seat close to the throne; respectful treatment of the envoy; remembrance of friends; closing the mission with satisfaction;--all these shall be noted as indicating the good graces of the enemy and the reverse his displeasure.

126 pratilomena sādhanaṃ viparyayaḥ

127 parasya vāci vaktre dṛṣṭyāṃ ca prasādaṃ vākyapūjanamiṣṭaparipraśnaṃ guṇakathāsaṅgamāsannamāsanaṃ satkāramiṣṭeṣu smaraṇaṃ viśvāsagamanaṃ ca lakṣayet tuṣṭasya, viparītamatuṣṭasya (arthaśā 1.16)

Explanation

The instructions for an envoy are provided above, emphasizing the importance of observing the reception they receive in the enemy's country. The underlined portion exemplifies the application of Viparyaya Tantrayuktis, where the enjoyable reception is described extensively, while for the non-pleasurable reception, only the term "reverse" is employed, representing the opposite of the aforementioned details. This concise approach effectively conveys the intended meaning without the need for explicit elaboration.

Example from Other texts

सावयवं परतन्त्रं व्यक्तं विपरीतमव्यक्तम् ॥[128]

(sāṅkhya-kārikā Verse 10)

Endowed with limbs, dependent is the manifest (Vyakta) and the reverse is the unmanifest (Avyakta).

Notes and Observations

As evident from the definition and illustration above Viparya Yuktis refers to inferring a reverse statement from a positive one. It involves structuring content intelligently and compactly within a thesis. Crafting statements in a manner where their reverse perfectly suits the opposite condition requires thoughtful consideration. Readers can appreciate the intricacy of expression when contrariety is skillfully employed. It adds depth and nuance to the thesis, enriching the reading experience.

Take Aways

For Researchers:

Be Mindful to effectively notice suitable occasion and apply this technique of crafting statements to convey the converse to display compactness and intelligence of structuring of the thesis.

128 sāvayavaṃ paratantraṃ vyaktaṃ viparītamavyaktam.. sāṅkhyakārikā ślokaḥ 10.

For Evaluators:

The presence of Viparyaya Yuktis (Coveying the converse) in a thesis indicates the writer's eye for subtlety and sophistication, hence Recognize this as a mark of the writer's adeptness in conveying complex ideas with precision.

Summary

This chapter explored the significance of twelve Tantrayuktis, in structuring the content of a thesis. It delved into Yuktis such as Adhikaraṇa, Vidhānam, Uddeśa, Nirdeśa, Pūrvapakṣa, Uttarapakṣa, Atikrāntāvekṣaṇa, Anāgatāvekṣaṇa, Pradeśa, Atideśa, Prasaṅga, and Viparya Yukti, highlighting their utility in creating a coherent and compelling narrative within a thesis.

1. **Adhikaraṇa Yukti:** This Yuktis serves the purpose and approach of a thesis established a framework for exploration, ensuring engagement and facilitating meaningful insights for both the author and the reader.
2. **Vidhāna Yukti:** The Table of Contents is a vital component in structuring a thesis, providing a roadmap for both the author's exploration and the evaluator's assessment.
3. **Uddeśa and Nirdeśa Yukti:** Uddeśa Yukti, focusing on concise statements at the outset of each topic, aids in micro-planning and enhanced memorization for readers. Nirdeśa Yuktis emphasizes systematic elaboration on brief statements or enumerated components, ensuring coherence between initial statements and subsequent elaborations. Together, these Yuktis form an essential pair in structuring the thesis, guiding the organization of knowledge and facilitating a clear and organized presentation of arguments or findings.
4. **Pūrvapakṣa Yuktis and Uttarapakṣa Yukti:** Addressing objections and their refutations strengthenes the research's

theoretical foundation, foster critical thinking, and enhance the credibility of the thesis.

5. **Atikrāntāvekṣaṇa Yukti, Anāgatāvekṣaṇa Yukti, Pradeśa Yukti, and Atideśa Yukti:** By referencing descriptions and applying rules from earlier contexts to later ones and vice versa, these Yuktis ensured a compact and coherent structure within the thesis, showcasing the researcher's intelligence and diligence.
6. **Prasaṅga Yukti:** This Yuktis emphasized the avoidance of repetition within the same section, promoting a concise structure while maintaining brevity and clarity.
7. **Viparya Yukti:** Inverting positive statements to convey reverse ideas facilitates compact structuring and fosters engagement and critical thinking among readers. The presence of Viparya Yuktis in a thesis reflects the writer's subtlety and precision in conveying complex ideas.

In conclusion, the Yuktis discussed in this section brings out the invaluable role of Tantrayuktis in structuring the content of a thesis, from establishing clear objectives to systematically addressing objections and refining arguments. Through the application of these logical devices, researchers will be able to construct compelling narratives that engaged readers and stand up to rigorous evaluation, ultimately contributing to the advancement of knowledge within their respective fields.

A SHORT QUIZ!

1. Which Tantrayuktis emphasizes the importance of concise statements at the beginning of each topic?

   a. Uddeśa Yukti
   b. Nirdeśa Yukti
   c. Vidhāna Yukti
   d. Adhikaraṇa Yukti

2. True or False: Addressing objections and their refutations strengthens the theoretical foundation of a thesis. (True/False)

3. Match the following Tantrayuktis with their descriptions:

   a. Pūrvapakṣa Yukti
   b. Pradeśa Yukti
   c. Viparya Yukti
   d. Atideśa Yukti

5. Uddeśa Yuktis focuses on __________ statements at the outset of each topic.

   a. Emphasizes avoiding repetition within the same section.
   b. Inverts positive statements to convey reverse ideas.
   c. Addresses objections and their refutations.
   d. Ensures a compact and coherent structure within the thesis by referencing descriptions and rules from earlier contexts.

Yuktis for Polishing Thesis Language

9 Yuktis

In crafting a thesis, the language utilized serves a multifaceted role, aiming to clarify, explain, inform, and invent. It acts as a vital tool for elucidating complex concepts and theories, ensuring readers comprehend the content with clarity. Through lucid explanations, the language unravels the rationale behind research methodologies, analytical frameworks, and empirical findings, fostering understanding and engagement. Furthermore, it serves as a conduit for disseminating factual information and scholarly insights, providing readers with a comprehensive understanding of the subject matter. Simultaneously, the language encourages inventive expression, allowing for the exploration of innovative ideas and interpretations within the academic discourse. By maintaining precision, objectivity, and creativity, the language of the thesis not only informs but also inspires further inquiry and intellectual exploration, contributing to the advancement of knowledge within the respective field.

There are nine Tantrayuktis which help a writer of thesis in the above aspects of brining about essential qualities of a language of a thesis.

The Nine Yuktis are as follows - पदार्थः, योगः, व्याख्यानम्, निर्वचनम्, उपमानम्, निदर्शनम्, वाक्यशेषः, अर्थापत्तिः and स्वसंज्ञा. [129]

Of these

- पदार्थः, योगः, व्याख्यानम्, निर्वचनम्, उपमानम्, निदर्शनम्[130] – Devices that help to Clarify and Explain.
- The Yuktis वाक्यशेषः, अर्थापत्तिः[131] help Imply and refine.
- And स्वसंज्ञा[132] helps Invention in language.

As earlier each of these will be defined, illustrated in this section. Their utility will also be discussed.

---

129 padārthaḥ, yogaḥ, vyākhyānam, nirvacanam, upamānam, nidarśanam, vākyaśeṣaḥ, arthāpattiḥ and svasaṃjñā.

130 padārthaḥ, yogaḥ, vyākhyānam, nirvacanam, upamānam, nidarśanam

131 vākyaśeṣaḥ, arthāpattiḥ

132 svasaṃjñā

1. पदार्थः Padārtha

Definition -

पदावधिकः अर्थः।[133]

The sense which a word has to convey is its meaning;

Illustration -

मूलहरः इति पदम्। "यः पितृपैतामहम् अर्थम् अन्यायेन भक्षयति सः मूलहरः[134]

(Kauṭilya Arthaśāstra 2.9)

The word mūlahara: "Whoever squanders the wealth acquired for him by his father and grandfather is a mūlahara, a prodigal son."

According to the etymological analysis of the term "Mūlahara," "Mūla" refers to the root and "hara" is the one who snatches or destroys. While it can have various meanings, the word's contextual meaning is clarified. Chapter 9 of Adhikaraṇa 2 of Kauṭilya Arthaśāstra deals with the "Examination of the Conduct of Government Servants." It has been stated that the government servant should be examined to determine whether he is a "Mūlahara" - a prodigal son who eats up the wealth of his forefathers. Hence, contextually confining and clarifying the meaning of the term is called "Padārtha," as evident from the illustration.

133 padāvadhikaḥ arthaḥ.

134 mūlaharaḥ iti padam. "yaḥ pitṛpaitāmaham artham anyāyena bhakṣayati saḥ mūlaharaḥ ". (arthaśā 2.9)

Examples from Other texts

'वेदोत्पत्तिमध्यायं व्याख्यास्याम 'इत्युक्ते सन्दिह्यते बुद्धिः- कतमस्य वेदस्योत्पत्तिं वक्ष्यतीति, यतः ऋग्वेदादयस्तु, वेदाः; 'विद विचारणे, विद्लृ लाभे, 'इत्येतयोश्च धात्वोरनेकार्थयोः प्रयोगात्, तत्र पूर्वापरयोगमुपलभ्य प्रतिपत्तिर्भवति- आयुर्वेदोत्पत्तिमयं विवक्षुरिति; एष पदार्थः [135]

(suśruta-saṃhitā 6.65.10)

"When it is said, 'Let us now explain about the chapter of genesis of the Veda,' the mind becomes doubtful—of which Veda the genesis will be discussed? Because there are Ṛgveda and other texts which are Vedas. 'Vid' to analyze, 'Vid' to attain are the verbal roots seen to have been used to denote many connotations. But upon seeing the earlier and later usages of the term (in the text), it becomes clear that the genesis of Āyurveda is being desired to be explained. This is Padārtha."

...गतासून् गतप्राणान् मृतान्, अगतासून् अगतप्राणान् जीवतश्च न अनुशोचन्ति पण्डिताः आत्मज्ञाः। पण्डा आत्मविषया बुद्धिः येषां ते हि पण्डिताः, 'पाण्डित्यं निर्विद्य' (बृ. उ. ३। ५। १) इति श्रुतेः। परमार्थतस्तु तान् नित्यान् अशोच्यान् अनुशोचसि, अतो मूढोऽसि इत्यभिप्रायः[136]

Śaṅkara Bhāṣya – Bhagavad-gītā (2.11)

Because, paṇḍita, the learned, the knowers of the Self panda means wisdon about the Self; those indeed who have this are paṇḍitah, one the authority of the Upaniṣadic *text, '॥.the knowers of Brahman, having known all about scholarship,॥.' (Br. 3.5.1) ['Therefore the*

135 'vedotpattimadhyāyaṃ vyākhyāsyāma' ityukte sandihyate buddhiḥ- katamasya vedasyotpattiṃ vakṣyatīti, yataḥ ṛgvedādayastu, vedāḥ; 'vida vicāraṇe, vidlṛ lābhe,' ityetayośca dhātvoranekārthayoḥ prayogāt, tatra pūrvāparayogamupalabhya pratipattirbhavati- āyurvedotpattimayaṃ vivakṣuriti; eṣa padārthaḥ

136 ...gatāsūn gataprāṇān mṛtān, agatāsūn agataprāṇān jīvataśca na anuśocanti paṇḍitāḥ ātmajñāḥ. paṇḍā ātmaviṣayā buddhiḥ yeṣāṃ te hi paṇḍitāḥ, 'pāṇḍityaṃ nirvidya' (bṛ. u. 3. 5. 1) iti śruteḥ. paramārthatastu tān nityān aśocyān anuśocasi, ato mūḍho'si ityabhiprāyaḥ.. 2.11..

knowers of Brahman, having known all about scholorship, should try to live upon that strength which comes of Knowledge; having known all about this strength as well as scholorship, he becomes meditative; having known all about both meditativeness and its opposite, he becomes a knower of Brahman.'] ;

It is interesting to note how Ācārya Śaṅkara has applied Padārtha Tantrayukti to clarify the meaning of the word Paṇḍita. While the word Paṇḍita, in a general sense, can indicate a scholar proficient in various subjects and skills, here, in the context of this śloka (2.11 Bhagavadgītā), it is clarified that Paṇḍita is the one who has the wisdom about the ātman.

Notes and Observations

In research communication, Padārtha Yuktis (clarifying the meaning of terms with contextual consciousness) plays a critical role in ensuring the accuracy, clarity, and effectiveness of the communication process:

Research often deals with complex concepts and specialized terminology. Clarifying the meaning of terms ensures that there is precision in communication, minimizing the risk of misunderstanding or misinterpretation among readers or listeners. Terms may have different meanings or nuances depending on the context in which they are used. By providing context along with term definitions, researchers help readers or listeners understand how the term applies within the specific domain or topic being discussed. Research findings are often disseminated to diverse audiences, including fellow researchers, policymakers, and the general public. By clarifying the meaning of terms within the appropriate context, researchers facilitate better understanding among different audience groups, regardless of their level of expertise in the subject matter. Clear and precise communication fosters trust and credibility in research. When researchers take the time to clarify the meaning of terms and provide context, they demonstrate a commitment to transparency and accuracy, which enhances the credibility of their work. Overall, Padārtha Tantrayuktis (clarifying the meaning of terms with context consciousness) is essential for effective research communication, as it promotes clarity, precision, comprehension, trust, and critical engagement with the research content.

Take Aways

For Researchers:

Clarify the meaning of terms and provide context to ensure precision in communication, minimizing the risk of misunderstanding or misinterpretation among readers or listeners.

For Evaluators:

Evaluate whether that terms used in the thesis are clearly defined and contextualized to maintain precision in communication, thereby minimizing the risk of misunderstanding or misinterpretation.

2. योगः Yoga

Definition -

वाक्ययोजना योगः[137]

The arrangement of sentence is employment[138]

Illustration -

चतुर्वर्णाश्रमो लोकः [139]

(Kauṭilya Arthaśāstra 1.4)

The people in the four Varṇas and in the four ***āśramas***

One has to look at the complete verse that has been given as an illustration for the definition of the Yuktis to understand it better. The full verse is as follows –

137 vākyayojanā yogaḥ

138 The translation of RP Kangle is taken here in place of Shamashastry which is more appropriate. Shamashastry translates the portion on Yoga as - Pointing out similar facts by the use of such words as 'These and the like,' is suggestion of similar facts; for example: "The world consisting of the four castes and the four religious divisions and the like.". As evident from the discussion above this is not what Kauṭilya intends by the Tantrayukti.

139 caturvarṇāśramo lokaḥ (arthaśā 1.4)

चतुर्वर्णाश्रमो लोको राज्ञा दण्डेन पालितः।
स्वधर्मकर्माभिरतो वर्तते स्वेषु वेश्मसु ॥[140]

This people (loka) consisting of four castes and four orders of religious life, when governed by the king with his sceptre, will keep to their respective paths, ever devotedly adhering to their respective duties and occupations.

Though the translation gives the flow of the meaning cogently when observed in the source verse - the subject in the above sentence is चतुर्वर्णाश्रमो लोक (*people (loka) consisting of four castes and four orders of religious life,*) and verb is in the last section of the verse with associated terms - वर्तते स्वेषु वेश्मसु (*will keep to their respective paths*) are quite apart – which does not lead to comprehension of the verse easily.

In between the subject and the verb there are many other terms which speak about the role of the king and also the Svadharma etc This Yuktis does the Yoga –joining the subject with the verb – thereby facilitating comprehension. This will also be evident from the following āyurvedic example also.

Example form other Texts

तैलं पिबेच्चामृतवल्लिनिम्बहंसाह्वयावृक्षकपिप्पलीभिः
सिद्धं बलाभ्यां च सदेवदारु हिताय नित्यं गलगण्डरोगे
तैलं पिबेत्_सिद्धमिति_सम्बन्धः।[141]

(suśruta-saṃhitā 4.18.47)

One should consume the oil that is prepared with Amṛtavallī, nimba, haṃsapadi, pippalī, balā, atibalā, and devadāru, which is beneficial

140 caturvarṇāśramo loko rājñā daṇḍena pālitaḥ.
svadharmakarmābhirato vartate sveṣu veśmasu..

141 tailaṃ pibeccāmṛtavallinimbahaṃsāhvayāvṛkṣakapippalībhiḥ
siddhaṃ balābhyāṃ ca sadevadāru hitāya nityaṃ galagaṇḍaroge (suśruta 4.18.47)
tailaṃ pibet siddhamiti sambandhaḥ.

in the Galagaṇḍa (goitre) disease (Suśruta-saṃhitā 4.18.47). The connection is to be seen between the terms taila and siddha.

In this Saṃskṛta verse, the terms “Taila” (oil) and “Siddha” (prepared) are separated from each other. When we examine the literal translation of the verse, the need for the application of Yoga Tantrayuktis becomes evident.

Literal translation: oil (Tailam) one should drink (pibet) with *pippalī amṛtavallī haṃsapadī, nimba,* (amṛtavallinimbahaṃsāhvayāvṛkṣaka-pippalībhiḥ). Prepared (siddhaṃ) by the two balas (balābhyam) and with Devadāru (sadevadāru), beneficial (Hitāya) always (nityaṃ) in Goitre disease (Galagaṇḍaroge).

It can be s een that the word Oil and Prepared is quite apart from each other and this disrupts comprehension. To facilitate understanding application of Yoga Tantrayuktis in the process of paraphrasing the terms - oil & prepared are connected with each other.

Notes and Observations

The utility of Yoga Tantrayuktis extends beyond metrical composition to prose content in current day theses. In complex research subjects, sentences may become convoluted with numerous clauses and phrases to ensure factual accuracy. The aim should be to simplify sentences and convey complex ideas in a clear and straightforward manner. It is an art to express intricate concepts using simple sentences. However, if the complexity of the concept requires the inclusion of multiple conditions or exceptions, efforts should be made to clarify the sense of the sentence then and there. Footnotes or explanatory notes can be added to connect phrases, clauses, subjects, verbs, adjectives, and nouns. In this way Yoga Tantrayuktis can be brought to effect.

Take Aways

For Researchers:

Read and reread the thesis content before finalizing. Ensure the intelligibility of the content and indentify setnences that need the application clarifications and simplifications.

For Evaluators:

Look for effort in language of the thesis to clarify the meaning of complex sentences towards enhancing the overall intelligibility of the thesis.

3. व्याख्यानम् Vyākhyānam

Definition -

अतिशयवर्णना व्याख्यानम्[142]

Description in detail is explanation

Illustration -

विशेषतश्च सङ्घानां सङ्घधर्मिणां च राजकुलानां द्यूतनिमित्तो भेदः; तन्निमित्तो विनाश इत्यसत्यग्रहः पापिष्ठतमो व्यसनानां तन्त्रदौर्बल्यादिति "

(Kauṭilya Arthaśāstra 8.3)

"Especially amongst assemblies and confederacies of kings possessing the characteristics of assemblies, quarrel is due to gambling ; and destruction of persons due to the quarrel. Hence, among evil propensities, gambling is the worst evil, since it renders the king powerless for activity."

Though this this is self evident, the quality that comes out through the elaboration is the repeated emphasis of the harmfulness of the gambling. The repeated useage of the terms such as *quarrel, destruction, renders the king powerless – highten the ill effect of gambling*

142 atiśayavarṇanā vyākhyānam

Example from other Texts:

Caraka-saṃhitā

पुनश्च धातुभेदेन चतुर्विंशतिकः स्मृतः।
मनो दशेन्द्रियाण्यर्थाः प्रकृतिश्चाष्टधातुकी॥[143]

(caraka-saṃhitā 4.1.17)

Puruṣa comprises of six dhatu (elements), viz. five mahabhuta (in their subtle form) and consciousness. The element of consciousness alone could also be considered puruṣa. [17]

The elaboration on the Puruṣa which starts in verse 17 contiues till verse 42.

In Verse 42 the discussion gets completed as follows:

न चेत् कारणमात्मा स्याद्भादयः स्युरहेतुकाः।
न चैषु सम्भवेज् ज्ञानं न च तैः स्यात् प्रयोजनम्॥[144]

(caraka-saṃhitā 4.1.42)

If Puruṣa is not recognized as a chief cause, then everything mentioned above will be considered as causeless. Then the theory of cause and effect which is a fundamental tenet of Āyurveda will fail and no one will put any effort in understanding the cause of any effect.

In the course of the discussion from 17-42 the componets that constitue the concept of Puruṣa including Manas/mind (20-21), Role of Buddhi/ intellect (22-24), Functions of Karmendiryas/Motor Organs (25 -26), Mahābhūtas/five elements (27-30), process of perception (32-34), **Rāśi-puruṣa** /hoilisitc human being (35 onwards) etc are discussed. [145]

---

143 punaśca dhātubhedena caturviṃśatikaḥ smṛtaḥ|
mano daśendriyāṇyarthāḥ prakṛtiścāṣṭadhātukī||caraka śarīrasthānam 1.17||

144 na cet kāraṇamātmā syādbhādayaḥ syurahetukāḥ|
na caiṣu sambhavej jñānaṃ na ca taiḥ syāt prayojanam|| caraka śarīrasthānam 1.42||

145 While discussion on Puruṣa continues in this chapter, the major compontes of Puruṣa are covered in range of verses 17-42 from śarīra-sthāna chapter 1.

Unlike the example from the Arthaśāstra, where elaboration was used for emphasis – here elaboration is used for detailing. Many aspects of Puruṣa/human being which is not generally understood is enumerated.

Notes and Observations

Vyākhyāna Yuktis (Elaboration) is one of the fundamental characteristic of a thesis language. Any original ideas or insights discovered through research need to be systematically and elaborately discussed to ensure effective communication of the contribution. While cryptic notes and aphorisms may have their place, they often fall short in conveying the depth and significance of the research findings. As seen in the example from Kauṭilya Arthaśāstra elaborations can be used to enhance the impact of various phenomena discussed within the thesis. As evident from Caraka-saṃhitā example - through elaboration, previously unknown details can be brought to light, enriching the understanding of the subject matter. Elaboration should serve specific purposes, such as elucidating complex concepts or shedding light on obscure aspects of the topic. The primary objective of elaboration should not be to make the thesis bulky. Instead, it should focus on enhancing clarity and depth of understanding. Unfortunately, many modern theoretical theses prioritize quantity over quality, leading to superficial elaboration.

Take Aways

For Researchers:

1. Ensure that your original ideas and insights are systematically and elaborately discussed to effectively communicate your contributions, enhancing clarity and depth of understanding.
2. Use elaboration to elucidate complex concepts and shed light on obscure aspects, avoiding superficiality and prioritizing quality over quantity in your thesis.

For Evaluators:

1. Observe whether the researcher thoroughly discuss their original ideas and insights, promoting clear and in-depth communication of their contributions.
2. Examine the use elaboration for explaining in complex concepts and illuminating obscure aspects, focusing on depth and quality rather than unnecessary length.

4. उपमानम् Upamāna

Definition -

दृष्टेनादृष्टस्य साधनम् उपमानम्[146]

Proving an unseen (thing or course of circumstances) by what has bee seen is simile;

Illustration -

निवृत्तपरिहारान् पितेव अनुगृह्णीयात्।[147]

(Kauṭilya Arthaśāstra 2.1)

He shall regard with fatherly kindness those who have passed the period of remission of taxes.

During the establishment of new settlements or during other critical moments, taxes will be waived. The king is expected to show paternal kindness towards those who have completed their tax exemption period. While the relationship between a father and his children is well understood, what remains unclear is how a king should treat subjects who have just finished their tax holidays, earned through their service in setting up new settlements. Should the king immediately impose taxes harshly, or should he show leniency initially? This question is clarified through the use of an analogy or simile.

146 dṛṣṭenādṛṣṭasya sādhanam upamānam

147 nivṛttaparihārān piteva anugṛhṇīyāt. (arthaśā 2.1)

Example from other texts

यथा वस्त्राणां स्थूलो मलः पूर्वं निर्धूयते पश्चात्सूक्ष्मो यत्नेनोपायेन चापनीयते तथा स्वल्पप्रतिपक्षाः स्थूला वृत्तयः क्लेशानां, सूक्ष्मास्तु महाप्रतिपक्षा इति [148]

(Yogasūtra-vyāsabhāṣyam 2.11)

Just as the dust in a piece of cloth is at first shaken off, and the finer kinds then removed by finer means, — so in the same manner, the gross functions of the distractions have small adversaries, whereas the subtile ones have great adversaries.

As evident from the example – the dust on the cloth and the method of its removal is known and what is shown is the nature of the distractions of the mind gross and subtle and how to shake them off, which is not known.

Notes and Observations

Similes play a crucial role in thesis writing by clarifying unfamiliar concepts with familiar ones, enhancing understanding and effective concept transfer. Similes also captivate readers, fostering interest and aiding retention in thesis writing. They add vividness to prose, making it enjoyable to read. Memorable comparisons leave lasting impressions, reinforcing key concepts. A language rich in similes within a theoretical scientific subject not only reflects the researcher's confidence in their grasp of complex concepts but also demonstrates a mastery that resonates with the evaluator, showcasing clarity of thought and an ability to communicate intricate theories in a relatable and accessible manner.

148 yathā vastrāṇāṃ sthūlo malaḥ pūrvaṃ nirdhūyate paścātsūkṣmo yatnenopāyena cāpanīyate tathā svalpapratipakṣāḥ sthūlā vṛttayaḥ kleśānāṃ, sūkṣmāstu mahāpratipakṣā iti - yogasūtravyāsabhāṣyam 2.11

Take Aways

For Researchers:

Utilize similes to clarify unfamiliar concepts with familiar ones, enhancing understanding and effective concept transfer.

For Evaluators:

Look for the researcher's effort to use of any comparisions in the language to clarify unfamiliar concepts with familiar ones towards enhancing the quality of reseach communication.

5. निदर्शनम् Nidarśana

Definition -

दृष्टान्तो दृष्टान्तयुक्तो निदर्शनम्[149]

Exemplifying by means of an example is illustration[150]

Example -

विगृहीतो हि ज्यासा हस्तिना पादयुद्धम् इव अभ्युपैति

(Kauṭilya Arthaśāstra 7.6.6)

In war with a superior, the inferior will be reduced to the same condition as that of a foot-soldier fighting with an elephant

As evident from the above quote, illustrations vividly drive home the concept with great impact, though the concept being imparted is common place knowledge.

149 dṛṣṭānto dṛṣṭāntayukto nidarśanam

150 Translation of RP Kangle is better in this instance: https://archive.org/details/OdAH_artha-shastra-part-2-r.-p.-kangle/page/514/mode/2up?view=theater

Example from other Texts

यथा विषं यथा शस्त्रं यथाग्निरशनिर्यथा।
तथौषधमविज्ञातं विज्ञातममृतं यथा' ||[151]

(caraka-saṃhitā 1.1.115)

Medicine (the method of utilization of) which is not know is like a poison, weapon, fire or lightning. But if it is known it is like nectar.

Notes and Observations

Nidarśana vis a vis Upamāna: While sharing similarities with Upamāna Tantrayuktis, Nidarśana primarily serves as illustration rather than revealing the unknown through the known. It creates word pictures for enhanced clarity and driving home key messages effectively. For example, Kauṭilya 's analogy of a footsoldier facing an elephant vividly illustrates the certain negative consequences of misadventure, despite the outcome being familiar. So does the example from Caraka-saṃhitā.

The Take Aways are similar to the previous Tantrayuktis.

151 yathā viṣaṃ yathā śastraṃ yathāgniraśaniryathā.
tathauṣadhamavijñātaṃ vijñātamamṛtaṃ yathā'..
(caraka-saṃhitā sūtrasthāna 1:125)

6. निर्वचनम् Nirvacana

Definition -

संज्ञयोक्तस्य तदर्थेन सह योजनम्।[152]

Stating the derivative sense of a word, is derivation

Illustration -

व्यस्यत्येनं श्रेयसः इति व्यसनम्।[153]

(Kauṭilya Arthaśāstra 8.1)

That which throws off (vyasyati) a king from his prosperous career is propensity (vyasana).

Adhikaraṇa 8 chapter 1 is about "The aggregate of the calamities of the elements of sovereignty". Right at the outset Kauṭilya establishes the meaning of the term. In the very first few lines of the chapter he states –

When calamities happen together, the form of consideration should be whether it is easier to take an offensive or defensive attitude. National calamities, coming from Providence or from man happen from one's misfortune or bad policy. The word vyasana (vices or calamities), means the reverse or absence of virtue, the preponderance of vices, and occasional troubles. That which deprives (vyasyati) a person of his happiness is termed vyasana (vices or calamities).

152 saṃjñayoktasya tadarthena saha yojanam

153 vyasyatyenaṃ śreyasaḥ iti vyasanam. - vyasanam (arthaśā 8.1)

The underlined portion is the etymology/derivation of the term. By this Yuktis the protocol of establishing the derivative meaning of the term is done, which minimizes the possibility of fanciful interpretations or misinterpretations.

Example from other text

Many Saṃskṛta texts use Nirvacana Tantrayuktis (etymological derviations). Some examples are as follows -

आयुर्विद्यते अस्मिन्, अनेन वा आयुर्विन्दतीति - आयुर्वेदः[154]

(Suśruta-saṃhitā 6.65.35)

That in which āyus (longevity exists) or that by which longevity is achieved is Āyurveda

समाधीयते चित्तमस्मिन्निति समाधिः[155]

(Bhagavadgītā-śāṅkara-bhāṣya 2,53)

That (state) in which the mind gets settled is called as Samādhi

सम्प्रसाद इति सुषुप्तं स्थानमुच्यते; सम्यक्प्रसीदत्यस्मिन्निति निर्वचनात्[156]

(Brahmasūtra-śāṅkara-bhāṣya 1.3.8)

Samprasāda refers to deep sleep; as that is the state of pleasentness and clarity

Notes and observations

The necessity of including etymological derivations in a research thesis depends on the specific context and requirements of the study. In some cases, especially in fields where understanding the historical development of terminology is crucial, such as linguistics or historical studies, etymological derivations can be used. They may

154 āyurvidyate asmin, anena vā āyurvindatīti - āyurvedaḥ

155 samādhīyate cittamasminniti samādhiḥ

156 samprasāda iti suṣuptaṃ sthānamucyate; samyakprasīdatyasminniti nirvacanāt

help demonstrate the evolution of concepts or terms over time and enrich the reader's understanding of the subject matter. However, in other fields where etymology is not directly relevant to the research, extensive etymological discussions may not be necessary. In such cases, it's important for the researcher to prioritize clarity, relevance, and consciousness in presenting their finding as well as the expectations of the academic community in the relevant field. But texts of Indian Knowledge systems in Saṃskṛta, often provide etymological derivations for several reasons. It may also include -

a) Providing Linguistic and Cultural Context: Etymological derivations clarify word meanings by tracing historical roots and provide cultural and linguistic context to the terms and concepts under discussion. b) Interpretative Depth: Etymological also offers interpretative insights into the intended meaning within a particular context by providing various options of derivations and meanings. This approach deepens the reader's understanding of language and enhances comprehension of the text's underlying nuances. Thus, as evident, it is a useful tool that adds depth to the language of a thesis.

Take Aways

For Researchers:

Include etymological derivations to enhance understanding, clarify meanings, enrich analysis, and demonstrate thorough research and deep engagement with the subject.

For Evaluators:

Look for etymological derivations, as they enhance understanding, clarify meanings, enrich analysis, and demonstrate thorough research and deep engagement with the subject.

7. वाक्यशेषः Vākyaśeṣa

Definition -

येन वाक्यं समाप्यते स वाक्यशेषः[157]

That portion of a sentence which is omitted, though necessary to convey a complete sense, is ellipsis

Illustration -

छिन्नपक्षस्येव राज्ञः चेष्टानाशश्च। तत्र शकुनेरिति वाक्यशेषः[158]

(Kauṭilya Arthaśāstra 8.1)

"With his feathers plucked off, he will lose his power to move." Here 'like a bird' is omitted (ellipsis)

In the chapter on the calamities that might befall a kingdom (8.1), Bharadvāja asserts that if the minister is affected, then the king is greatly affected. The distress of the minister will incapacitate the king, likened to a bird losing its wings. However, the word "bird" is omitted in the sentence above.

157 yena vākyaṃ samāpyate sa vākyaśeṣaḥ
158 chinnapakṣasyeva rājñaḥ ceṣṭānāśaśca. tatra śakuneriti vākyaśeṣaḥ

Examples from other texts

Caraka-saṃhitā

"प्रवृत्तिर्हेतुभावानां" (सू.अ.१६) इत्यत्र 'अस्ति' इति पदं पूर्यते,[159]

(āyurvedadīpikā (caraka-saṃhitā) 8.12.42)

In the verse pravṛttirhetubhāvānāṃ the (obvious)word asti (is) supplied to complete the sentence.

To explain – in the 16th chapter of Sūtra-sthana of caraka-saṃhitā (verse 28)- theory of natural destruction is being explaind. There we find the following verse –

प्रवृत्तिहेतुर्भावानां न निरोधेऽस्ति कारणम्।
केचित्तत्रापि मन्यन्ते हेतुं हेतोरवर्तनम्।[160]

There is always a reason for the existence of beings, but none exists for their annihilation. However, some scholars argue that the cessation of their causal factors is what causes their annihilation.

In the verse above, it is noteworthy that the word asti (exists) is not explicitly used in connection with the cause of existence of beings (pravṛttihetu). However, it is explicitly used with nirodha (annihilation). This omission indicates the use of ellipsis, and one must understand that the word asti (there is a cause of existence) should also be inferred in relation to pravṛttihetu.

Notes and observations

The following aspects can be noted with regard to employment of Vākyaśeṣa in the language of a thesis -

159 "pravṛttirhetubhāvānāṃ" (sū.a.16) ityatra 'asti' iti padaṃ pūryate, (āyurvedadīpikā carakasaṃhitā siddhisthānaṃ 12.42)

160 pravṛttiheturbhāvānāṃ na nirodhe'sti kāraṇam|
kecittatrāpi manyante hetuṃ hetorāvartanam ||28||

1. Refinement: Vākyaśeṣa aids in refining language by omitting redundant or obvious words, thereby streamlining the expression. In a thesis, where clarity and conciseness are paramount, ellipsis helps to maintain a scholarly tone.
2. Focus on Essential Content: Vākyāśeṣa directs attention to key arguments, ensuring reader engagement.
3. Decodability: It is essential to use ellipsis correctly to maintain readability and ensure the easy decoding of the intended meaning. Overuse or improper application of ellipsis can lead to confusion or ambiguity in the text. Therefore, it is crucial for thesis writers to exercise discretion and avoid omitting vital words that are necessary for clarity and coherence.

Take Aways

For Reseachers:

As a researcher, use ellipsis judiciously to demonstrate your commitment to quality language, thereby enhancing your thesis's professionalism.

For Evaluators:

Recognize judicious use of ellipsis as evidence of the writer's commitment to quality language, enhancing the thesis's professionalism.

8. अर्थापत्तिः Arthāpatti

Definition -

यदुक्तमर्थादापद्यते सार्थापत्तिः[161]

What naturally follows from a statement of facts, though not spoken of in plain terms, is implication

Example -

"लोकयात्राविद् राजानमात्मद्रव्यप्रकृतिसम्पन्नं
प्रियहितद्वारेणाश्रयेत **(5.4.1)**"
नाप्रियहितद्वारेणाश्रयेतेत्यर्थादापन्नं भवतीति।[162]

(Kauṭilya Arthaśāstra 15)

One conversant with the ways of the world should resort to a king endowed with personal excellences and the excellences of material constituents through such as are dear and beneficial (to the king).' (5.4.1) 81 That he should not resort through one who is not dear and beneficial follows as a matter of course.

As illustrated, it is explicitly stated that one should approach the king "through those who are dear and beneficial to him." The implication is

161 yaduktamarthādāpadyate sārthāpattiḥ

162 "lokayātrāvid rājānamātmadravyaprakṛtisampannaṃ priyahitadvāreṇāśrayeta" (adhi0 5. adhyā0 4)
nāpriyahitadvāreṇāśrayetetyarthādāpannaṃ bhavatīti.

that one should not seek access through individuals who are not held in high regard or beneficial to the king.

Example from other Texts

ओदनं भोक्ष्ये इत्युक्ते अर्थादापन्नं भवति नायं पिपासुर्यवागूमिति।[163]

(suśruta-saṃhitā 6.64.20)

"I will eat rice" if this is said, then the implication is he is not desirous of driniking porridge.

The patient's preferences, such as expressing a desire for rice over porridge, serve as indicators of changes in appetite. Caregivers should be attentive to such cues and adjust the patient's diet and medication accordingly. It's important to recognize that patients may not always explicitly express all their preferences due to pain and other health conditions.

Notes and Observations

The following are the observations on Arthāpatti (Implication) based on the definition and illustrations that have been discussed –

a) Enhanced Communication: Arthāpatti allows for the communication of implicit meanings, enriching the depth of expression by conveying nuances effectively and also showcases sophisticated use of language by the thesis writer. b) Subtle Interpretations in practice: Arthāpatti is not only useful in text construction as a language refinement tool. As shown from the Suśruta-saṃhitā example, even in care giving the need to employ Arthāpatti is brought out. c) Need for Balance: However, it is crucial for writers to use Arthāpatti judiciously to maintain clarity, especially in situations necessitating explicit communication.

163 odanaṃ bhokṣye ityukte arthādāpannaṃ bhavati nāyaṃ pipāsuryavāgūmiti. (suśrutasaṃhitā 6.65.20)

Take Aways

For the Researcher:

Ensure to use implication to convey what naturally follows from a statement of facts, even if not spoken of in plain terms.

For the Reviewer:

Identify how implications are used to reveal the underlying meaning from statements of fact, even when not directly articulated.

9. स्वसंज्ञा Svasaṃjñā

Definition -

परैः असंमितः शब्दः स्वसंज्ञा।[164]

Words which are not used by others in the special sense in which they are used by the author are his own technical terms

Illustration -

प्रथमा प्रकृतिस्तस्य भूम्यनन्तरा द्वितीया भूम्येकान्तरा तृतीया इति [165]

(Kauṭilya Arthaśāstra 6.2)

"He who is close to the conqueror's territory is the first member); next to him comes the second member (Bhumyanantarā; and next to the second comes the third (Bhumyekāntara).

In the chapter concerning peace and effort, which discusses the endeavor (Vyayāma) to achieve results for the country and ensuring undisturbed enjoyment (śarma) of those results, Kauṭilya teaches about the role of neighboring kings in either supporting or hindering peace and industry. In this context, Kauṭilya introduces the terms "Bhumyanantarā" and "Bhumyekāntara" as examples of Svasaṃjñā Tantrayuktis in the 15th Adhikaraṇa.

---

164 paraiḥ asaṃmitaḥ śabdaḥ svasaṃjñā.

165 bhūmyantarā (svabhūmyavyavahitā bhūmiḥ,), bhūmyekāntarā (deśenaikena vyavahitā) (arthaśā 6.2)

Example from other Texts

यथा- जेन्ताकहोलाकादिका सञ्ज्ञा[166]

(Caraka-saṃhitā 8. 12..41-45)

In Āyurveda dīpikā a commentary on Caraka-saṃhitā Cakrapāṇidatta gives the above examples for Svasaṃjñā in the text. Jentāka refers to a heated underground cellar (Caraka-saṃhitā 1.14.46) and holaka (Caraka-saṃhitā 1.14.63) – a method of sudation where the beadsted of a patient is placed over burnt smokeless dung of specififed animals. These are the procedures that are detailed in Caraka-saṃhitā for the svedana treatment (sudation treatment) – which is considered an essential prerequisite for Pañca-karma therapy.

Notes and Observation

The following are some obsercations with regard to this Yuktis -

a) Introduction of Technical Terms**:** Authors can introduce technical terms unique to their work, either not known in other texts or used differently in general literature. This encourages researchers to employ "Svasaṃjñā" to denote concepts or processes specific to their text, ensuring ease of reference. b) Clarity Through Definition**:** While utilizing unique expressions, it's crucial to define the technical terms to avoid confusion. Clear definitions help readers understand the intended meaning and prevent misinterpretation. c)Examples from Saṃskṛta Literature**:** In Saṃskṛta literature we see words such as "Guṇas" and "Dh**ā**tu," which have specific meanings in different disciplines. These can be considered as instances of "Svasaṃjñā," as they denote specialized concepts within their respective fields. d) Invention or Attribution of New Meanings: In the examples given above Kauṭilya and Caraka seem to introduce new terms rather than attributing new meanings to existing ones in their literature. This suggests that researchers are encouraged to invent new terminologies. Thus, from a language perspective, this

166 yathā- jentākaholākādikā sañjñā - CS 8.12.41-45

Yuktis helps thesis writers towards effective communication and clarity in conveying their findings to the readers and evaluators.

Take Aways

For the Researcher:

Create and clearly define your own technical terms when using words in a special sense not commonly employed by others.

For the Reviewer:

Identify and assess any technical term that the author has uniquely defined or used in a special sense not found in common usage.

Summary

The nine Yuktis discussed in the chapter can be summarized under three heads – Yuktis to clarify, Yuktis to imply and Yuktis to invent. The salient points discussed are summarized hereunder –

Yukti to Clarify:

Under this head we can see Padārtha, Yoga, Nirvacana, Vyākhyāna, Upamāna and Nidarśanaa

1. Padārtha Yuktis (Clarifying Meaning with Context- Consciousness):

- Ensures precision and clarity in communication by defining terms within relevant context and Facilitates comprehension by providing contextual relevance to terms, minimizing ambiguity.
- Enhances credibility and trust in research communication through clear definitions and contextual explanations.

2. Yoga Tantrayuktis (Connecting the sentences):

- Helps in demystify complex expression with multiple phrases and clauses by paraphrasing the content
- Reading and rereading the thesis alone can bring out areas which require paraphrasinging or explanatory notes
- Evaluators can note the application of Yoga Tantrayuktis as the manifestation of the effort of the thesis writer to make the thesis intelligible

3. Nirvacana Yuktis (Etymological Derivations)

- In certain fields like linguistics or historical studies, etymological derivations clarify word meanings and provide cultural and linguistic context and demonstrate the historical evolution of terminology, enriching the reader's understanding and adding depth to the language of the thesis.
- Nirvacana offers interpretative depth by presenting various derivations and meanings, enhancing comprehension of underlying nuances, however, in other fields, researchers should prioritize clarity and conciseness, aligning with the expectations of the academic community.

4. Vyākhyāna Yuktis (Elaborating on Original Ideas):

- Systematically elaborates on original ideas to ensure effective communication of contributions and enhances the impact of various phenomena discussed within the thesis by providing detailed explanations.
- Reveals previously unknown details, enriching the understanding of the subject matter and contributing to scholarly discourse.

5. Upamāna Tantrayuktis (Utilizing Similes for Enhanced Communication):

- Clarifies obscure concepts with familiar comparisons, aiding in concept transfer and captivates readers and enhances engagement by employing vivid similes.
- Reflects the writer's ability to communicate complex theories in a relatable manner, enhancing the overall quality of the thesis.

6. Nidarśana Tantrayuktis (Illustrating Concepts for Clarity):

- Uses illustrations to enhance clarity and reinforce key messages effectively.
- Supplements textual explanations with visual aids to drive home complex concepts more effectively.

It's apparent from the above observations that these six Yuktis can be neatly categorized into three pairs. The first pair, Padārtha and Yoga, work together to connect words and sentences contextually, ensuring coherence in language. The second pair, Nirvacana and Vyākhyāna, contribute to elaboration and explanation, enriching the content with detailed insights. Finally, the third pair, Upamāna and Nidarśanaa, serve as tools for illustrations, enhancing clarity through vivid examples and comparisons. This grouping highlights how these Yuktis collectively enhance the clarity and coherence of language in a thesis.

Yukti to Imply

(Under this we can see two Yuktis Arthāpatti and Vākyaśeṣa)

7. Arthāpatti (Implication):

- Communicates implicit meanings effectively, enriching the depth of expression.
- Encourages critical engagement by subtly conveying nuanced ideas and insights.
- Balances implicit and explicit communication to elevate the intelligence and effectiveness of the language in the thesis.

8. Vākyaśeṣa (Utilizing Ellipsis for Language Refinement):

- Refines language by omitting redundant or obvious words, maintaining a scholarly tone.
- Directs attention to key arguments and ensures reader engagement.
- Requires judicious use to maintain readability and clarity, avoiding confusion or ambiguity.

Here, it's evident that while Arthāpatti Yuktis (Implication) operates at the level of implying meaning, Vākyaśeṣa Yuktis (Ellipsis) operates at the level of implying words that are explicitly not mentioned. This adds refinement to the language of the thesis.

Yukti for Inventing:

(Under this head we can see the Svasaṃjñā Tantrayuktis)

9. Svasaṃjñā (Inventing New Terminologies):

- Encourages the invention of new terminologies to denote unique concepts or processes unravelled in the thesis. This requires clear definitions to avoid confusion and ensure effective communication.
- Allows researchers to refine language by attributing new meanings to existing expressions or coining new terms as necessary.

Thus, by employing a range of Tantrayuktis, researchers can refine language in a thesis, ensuring clarity, precision, and effectiveness in communication. These linguistic devices serve as valuable tools for enhancing the overall quality and impact of research discourse.

In Conclusion, the 11 Yuktis for Developing Scholarly Content creation, 12 Yuktis for structuring the thesis, and 9 Yuktis to focus on the linguistic aspects convey the fundamental principles of thesis planning and execution. As discussed with illustrations, these methodologies are applicable across disciplines within Indian Knowledge Systems (IKS). Moreover, being universal in nature, they can be effectively applied in non-IKS contexts as well. When combined with modern works like the *MLA Handbook for Writers of Research Papers*, these Tantrayukti comprehensively cover almost all aspects of thesis and research paper construction and expression. They are not only valuable for researchers but also serve as a resource for evaluators of theses. Additionally, research supervisors or guides can progressively use these tools to mentor PhD candidates, ensuring the successful completion of their research endeavors.

Activity

Apply the Yuktis Arthāpatti and derive the implication of this paragraph

In a bustling city, an old tree stood tall amidst towering skyscrapers. Each year, its leaves would turn golden in the fall, casting a warm glow over the neighborhood. Despite its age and the urbanization around it, the tree thrived, offering shade to passersby and shelter to birds. The city council often discussed plans to modernize the area, yet the tree remained untouched, revered by the community. Its roots ran deep, unseen yet essential, holding the soil together

Given below is a paragraph with redundant expression. Applying Tantrayuktis Vākyaśeṣa and tighten the expression

The big giant tree stood tall in the forest.
The meeting will start at 10 AM in the morning.
She made a brief summary of the report.
We need to cooperate together to complete the project.
He returned back to his hometown after many years.

Identify the Svasaṃjñās in this paragraph

Yoga has long been recognized as a powerful practice for enhancing mental health. Through a combination of physical postures, breath control, and meditation, yoga provides a holistic approach to managing stress and anxiety. Regular practice of yoga can help reduce cortisol levels, the body's primary stress hormone, leading to a calmer and more balanced state of mind. Techniques like *prāṇāyāma* (breathing exercises) can improve oxygen flow to the brain, enhancing mental clarity and focus. Meditation practices such as *dhyāna* can help in cultivating mindfulness, promoting a deeper awareness of the present moment and reducing symptoms of depression. Additionally, the practice of *āsanas* (physical postures) not only strengthens the body but also releases tension stored in muscles, contributing to overall mental well-being. By integrating yoga into daily routines, individuals can experience a significant improvement in their mental health, leading to a more peaceful and centered life.

Chapter 5

Integrating Tantrayuktis in Thesis Review Processes

Tantrayuktis based Checklists & Grading

Building upon the foundation established in the previous chapter, which focused on the use of Tantrayuktis for refining content, structure, and language in thesis construction, we outlined how these methodologies guide the creation of well-organized, precise, and clear academic work. The 11 Yuktis for Developing Scholarly Content ensure comprehensive research, the 12 Yuktis for structure provide a coherent framework, and the 9 Yuktis for language enhance clarity and effectiveness in expression.

Based on this foundation, three documents tailored for academic research, particularly in the fields of Saṃskṛta and Indic Knowledge Systems (IKS) is presented hereunder. If successful, this framework can be expanded to other disciplines. These documents aim to offer a standardized approach to content creation, structuring, and language refinement for both researchers and evaluators. The proposed documents are as follows:

- Bhāratīya Śodha Sattva Sampat: A checklist based on Tantrayuktis for the content of a thesis, ensuring that the research question, objectives, and findings align with the principles of substantive inquiry.
- Bhāratīya Śodha Sāhitya Saṃracanā Prarūpa : A checklist for the structure of a thesis, guiding researchers on how to

systematically organize their arguments and findings in a coherent manner.

- Bhāratīya Śodha Sāhitya Bhāsha Bindu: A set of guidelines for refining the language used in a thesis, based on the devices that focus on linguistic clarity and precision.

Bhāratīya Śodha Sattva Sampat

This is a klist of five basic questions (Pañcapadī) that a researcher can look into with regard to the content of the thesis. The five questions of the checklist and the Yuktis from which they have been derived are given as follows[167] –

1. Does your thesis have a valid/useful research question? M (Saṃśaya)
2. Have you done systematic literature review and identified the gaps? M (apadeśa)
3. Have you quoted from the works of others with proper acknowledgement - to agree or disagree? M (Anumata)

Have you examined the validity & Soundness of the reasons/arguments that you have adduced in various portions of the thesis (Hetvartha/ Hetvābhāsa) M

4. What is the nature of your original contribution – New Suggestions in the chosen field (Upadeśa) Observations/creation on phenomena/rules with or without exceptions, optional rules, combination of factors, with provision for context specific interpretations (niyoga, ekānta, vikalpa, samuccaya, Ūhya) M

Thus, these Pañcapadī checklists, derived from traditional commentaries, can serve as a robust framework for academic writing. They ensure that research questions are valid, literature reviews are thorough, and

167 The letter M that appears in the five questions below refers to Mandatory. I shall be noted that in later sets of questions along with M, D (desirable) is also given.

the thesis is both systematically organized and linguistically refined, without deviating from the core meaning of the Yukti.

In the context of content evaluation also, evaluators can apply the same checklist to check the quality of the thesis.

Bhāratīya Śodha Sāhitya Samracanā Prarūpa:

When it comes to structuring a thesis, the application of Tantrayuktis provides a precise and comprehensive framework for organization. This approach, which we shall term, the Bhāratīya Śodha Sāhitya Samracanā Prārūpa, can be broken down into a Saptapadii, a seven-point checklist derived from twelve key Tantrayuktis. These seven points ensure that the structure of the thesis is well-defined, logically organized, and cohesive.

The 7 questions and the corresponding Yuktis are given below with a mark of M or D where M stands for Mandatory and D stands for desirable -

1. Do you have a well defined thesis title? (Adhikaraṇa) M
2. Do you have a table of contents? (Vidhāna) M
3. Have you listed and elaborated the topics systematically? (Uddeśa, nirdeśa) M
4. Have you systematically stacked the arguments against and for your thesis? (Pūrvapakṣa-uttarapakṣa) M

Have you tightened your thesis by hyperlinking discussion? (Atikrānta-Anāgatavekṣā) M

5. Have you optimized the utilization of the rules/logics/arguments created? (atideśa-pradeśa) D
6. Have you optimized the volume of the thesis text by using techniques of stating the converse and Same as above? D

Mandatory and Desirable Elements: Out of these seven points, the first five can be categorised as—Title, Table of Contents, Listing and Elaboration of Topics, Arguments For and Against, and Hyperlinking

Relevant Discussions—as mandatory. These form the backbone of a well-structured thesis and are critical to its clarity and coherence.

The last two points—Optimizing Rules and Logic and Stating the Converse/Using Ditto—are desirable. While they are excellent tools for enhancing the quality and compactness of the thesis, they may require a higher level of analytical thinking and mastery of the subject matter. Not every researcher will implement these, but doing so significantly improves the thesis's sophistication.

As earlier, the same aspects can by used by evaluators to check the structure of the thesis. By applying these criteria, evaluators can more objectively determine the quality and coherence of a thesis. This dual application for both researchers and evaluators enhances academic rigor and ensures that the structure of a thesis is as robust and effective as possible.

Bhāsha Bindu Saptapadī:

Bhāsha Bindu Saptapadī, focuses on the aspects of language (Bhāsha) that need to be taken care of while writing a thesis. This checklist, grounded in the Tantrayuktis framework, guides the researcher in refining the language of the thesis to ensure clarity, precision, and creativity.

The framework divides the roles of language into three key functions:

- Clarify and Explain
- Imply and Refine
- Invent and Innovate

Based on these functions, a (Bhāsha Saptapadī) (seven-point checklist) is developed using nine relevant Tantrayuktis. These points serve as a checklist for ensuring that the language used in a thesis is both effective and impactful.

Checklist for Language (Bhāsha Bindu Saptapadī)

1. Does your thesis clarify contextual meanings of the technical terms used (Padārtha) M
2. Does the Language of your thesis paraphrase and clarify meanings of the passages (Yoga) M
3. Does the language of your thesis elaborate on intricate topics in a justified manner (Vyakhya) M
4. Does the language of the thesis employ similes and examples to explain concepts (Nidarśanaa & Upamāna) M
5. Have you attempted to avoid verbosity in the language of the thesis by employing ellipsis and implications (Vākyaśeṣa & Arthāpatti) M
6. Does the language of the thesis employ etymological derivations to clarify terms (Nirvacana) D
7. Have you justifiably coined any new term to express your innovation and findings (svasaṃjñā) D

Mandatory and Desirable Elements: As earlier here also Mandatory and desirable elements can be seen in the check list. Clarifying contextual meanings, Paraphrasing and Clarifying ideas, Elaborating on intricate topics, and Explaining implicit meanings are mandatory. These ensure that the thesis is clear, comprehensible, and appropriately detailed. Conveying complex relationships, Using inference, and Allowing creativity and innovation are desirable. These elements elevate the quality of the thesis by adding depth, insight, and originality.Similar to the structuring checklist, this Bhāsha Bindu Saptapadī can be adapted for evaluators as well.

This checklist helps both the researcher and evaluator ensure that the language used in the thesis fulfills its purpose—making the thesis not only informative but also engaging.

Grading system based on the Check lists

The Tantrayuktis-inspired grading system provides a structured and quantifiable framework for thesis assessment. Notably, the first three checklists form the basis for grading, while the Do's and Don'ts section serves as a supplementary guide, offering valuable insights for both researchers and evaluators. However, the latter is not factored into the grading process.

Grading Breakdown:

- Content-related parameters (5 checklist questions): 10 marks each, totalling 50 marks.
- Structure-related parameters (7 checklist questions): 5 marks each, first 5 are mandatory, contributing 25 marks. (The remaining 2 are desirable, potentially adding additional marks if fulfilled)
- Language-related parameters (7 checklists): 5 marks each. First 5 are mandatory, contributing 25 marks. (The last 2 are desirable and may add further marks.)

Thus, a typical thesis would be graded out of 100 marks, but there is potential for an additional 20 marks (for fulfilling the desirable criteria), bringing the maximum score to 120 marks.

Suggested Grading Scale:

Above 100 (up to 120): Highly recommended – Represents an exemplary thesis that not only meets all mandatory criteria but also excels by fulfilling the desirable criteria. This could be adjudicated as one of the best theses.

90 to 100: Recommended – A solid and well-rounded thesis that meets all mandatory criteria. This level is suitable for publication or advanced recommendations without significant revisions.

70 to 90: Minor revisions – The thesis has potential but requires minor improvements. The grading system makes these revisions pointed and specific, offering constructive feedback to the researcher.

Less than 70: Major revisions – The thesis does not meet key standards and needs substantial work before being reconsidered for approval.

Benefits of this Grading System:

Clarity and Transparency: The criteria are specific and quantifiable, allowing both the researcher and evaluator to understand exactly what is expected. This minimizes ambiguity and subjective judgments.

Efficiency for Evaluators: Professors and scholars often juggle numerous responsibilities, and the time required to review a thesis can be significant. By focusing on these 19 essential aspects, this system ensures a thorough evaluation that is time-efficient and aligns with IKS principles. It helps evaluators offer pointed feedback rather than general comments, making the process more precise.

Informed Revisions: When revisions are necessary, the system provides specific, targeted areas for improvement based on the checklist. This makes the feedback more actionable and reduces vagueness often seen in traditional thesis reviews.

Integration of Traditional Wisdom with Modern Academia: This system, inspired by Tantrayuktis, not only adheres to Indian Knowledge Systems (IKS) but also ensures that these ancient methodologies are applied in a contemporary academic setting. By quantifying these parameters, it creates a bridge between ancient evaluative wisdom and modern research protocols.

Additional Considerations:

Incorporating the Checklist in Thesis Writing: As part of the thesis submission process, researchers could be required to show where they have applied the 19 steps within their work. This self-evaluation could also be part of the submission, ensuring that the thesis aligns with these criteria from the start.

Training for Evaluators and Researchers: To ensure this system is implemented consistently, there could be short courses or workshops for both researchers and evaluators on Tantrayuktis and their application in thesis writing and assessment. This would promote standardization and a shared understanding of the criteria.

Flexibility in the System: While the system is rigorous, it also allows for flexibility by incorporating desirable criteria that are not mandatory. This flexibility encourages innovation and creativity in research without penalizing those who may not need or be able to fulfill these higher-level criteria.

Integrating the Tantrayukti-based checklists into current day thesis writing and Evaluation

The idea of incorporating the above Pañchapādī and two Saptapadī Checklists into the methodology section of a thesis could be an efficient way to ensure that these aspects are systematically applied. By requiring researchers to highlight where they have used each Yuktis in their thesis (citing page numbers and examples), reflective research is promoted and it is ensured that the approach of the thesis writer is both structured and intentional.

Teaching Tantrayuktis and Implementing the Framework: The approach outlined herein can be integrated into educational programs as a module-based course on Tantrayuktis. Teaching researchers how to systematically apply these techniques, followed by assignments that allow them to demonstrate their use of Pañchapādī and Saptapadī in their own research areas, would build stronger foundations in scholarly writing.

Further, by making it mandatory for researchers to exhibit these steps in their thesis, this practice would:

- Strengthen the research methodology.
- Ensure a high standard of coherence, clarity, and innovation in academic writing.
- Encourage evaluators to engage with research more deeply, based on clearly defined criteria.

This system not only preserves the traditional wisdom embedded in Tantrayuktis but adapts it for contemporary research methodologies, making it a holistic and rigorous framework for both researchers and evaluators.

Chapter 6

Excellence and Pitfalls in Thesis Writing

Tantraguṇas and Tantradoṣas

The literature on Tantrayuktis also includes Tantraguṇas and Tantradoṣas. Tantraguṇa s point to virutes in thesis/text construction and Tantradoṣas point to flaws in text/thesis construction.

The list of Tantraguṇas[168] are found in the Vimānasasthāna of Caraka-saṃhitā (8th Chapter) verse 3.[169,170]

---

168 Though the term Tantraguṇa is not mentioned in this context of the quotation above Tantraguṇa is also not alien term to āyurveda-śāstra. In the aṣṭāṅga-hṛdaya uttara-tantra chapter 40 verse 78 we see the term Tantraguṇa being mentioned - इति तन्त्रगुणैर्युक्तं तन्त्रदोषविवर्जितम् iti tantraguṇairyuktaṃ tantradoṣavivarjitam. Dr WK lele also mentions these as Tantraguṇas (2004) (Pg.241). Also see a research article on Tantraguṇas - https://www.ncbi.nlm.nih.gov/pmc/articles/PMC5822987/)

169 विविधानि हि शास्त्राणि भिषजां प्रचरन्ति लोके; तत्र यन्मन्येत सुमहद्यशस्विधीर पुरुषासेवितमर्थबहुलमाप्तजनपूजितं त्रिविधशिष्यबुद्धिहितमपगतपुनरुक्तदोषमार्षं सुप्रणीतसूत्रभाष्यसङ्ग्रहक्रमं स्वाधारमनवपतितशब्दमकष्टशब्दं पुष्कलाभिधानं क्रमागतार्थमर्थतत्त्वविनिश्चयप्रधानं सङ्गतार्थमसङ्कुलप्रकरणमाशुप्रबोधकं लक्षणवच्चोदाहरणवच्च, तदभिप्रपद्येत शास्त्रम् vividhāni hi śāstrāṇi bhiṣajāṃ pracaranti loke; tatra yanmanyeta sumahadyaśasvidhīrapuruṣāsevitamarthabahulamāptajanapūjitaṃ trividhaśiṣyabuddhihitamapagatapunaruktadoṣamārṣaṃ supraṇītasūtrabhāṣyasaṅgrahakramaṃsvādhāramanavapatitaśabdamakaṣṭaśabdaṃ puṣkalābhidhānaṃ kramāgatārthamarthatattvaviniścayapradhānaṃ saṅgatārthamasaṅkulaprakaraṇamāśuprabodhakaṃ lakṣaṇavaccodāharaṇavacca, tadabhiprapadyeta śāstram

170 https://www.carakasamhitaonline.com/mediawiki-1.32.1/index.php?title=Rogabhishagjitiya_Vimana

The Tantraguṇa s (Characters) mentioned can be listed for easy comprehension as follows -

1. सुमहद् Sumahad – comprehensive (in size and content)
2. यशस्वी-धीरपुरुषसेवितम् Yaśasvī-dhīrapuruṣasevitam – consulted by the reputed and succesful
3. आप्तजनपूजितम् Āptajanapūjitam – revered by peers
4. अर्थबहुलम् Arthabahulam – rich in meaning
5. त्रिविधशिष्यबुद्धिहितम् trividhaśiṣyabuddhihitam – useful to all three types of learners (with good, moderate and poor intellect)
6. अपगतपुनरुक्तम् Apagatapunaruktam– non repetitive
7. आर्षम् Ārṣam – follows rishi tradition
8. सुप्रणीतसूत्रभाष्यक्रमम् Supraṇītasūtrabhāṣyakramam – follows briefing and elaboration systematically (well-structured and in good format)
9. स्वाधारम् Svādhāram – well evidenced
10. अनवपतितशब्दम् Anavapatitaśabdam – appropriate words (without vague and ambiguous language)
11. अकष्टशब्दम् Akaṣṭaśabdam – easy words
12. पुष्कलाभिधानम् Puṣkalābhidhānam – rich in synonyms, descrptions
13. क्रमगतार्थम् Kramagatārtham – sequential
14. अर्थतत्त्वविनिश्चयप्रधानम् Arthatattvaviniścayapradhānam – centered on establishing facts (focused on determination of objectives)
15. सङ्गतार्थम् Saṅgatārtham – endowed with logical flow
16. असङ्कुलप्रकरणम् Asaṅkulaprakaraṇam – without mixed up sections
17. आशुप्रबोधकम् Āśuprabodhakam – easy to understand
18. लक्षणवत् Lakṣaṇavat – endowed with definitions
19. उदाहरणवत् udāharaṇavat - endowed with illustrations

As evident from the above, these 19 points can also be classified into the categories of good characteristics of Content, strucuture and language of a thesis.

- Content: 1, 4,7,9, 14
- Structure: 6,8,13, 15,16
- Language: 10-12, 17-19 are varitures of good language in a thesis

Point 2,3 & 5 can be considered to have impact of all the three above.

Tantradoṣas

Tantradoṣas – flaws in composing a treatise - are found in the Sarvāṅgasundarī commentary on Aṣṭāṅga-hṛdaya in the uttara-tantra, in the 40 the section verse 78 there is a mention of Tantraguṇas and Tantradoṣas. In the Sarvāṅgasundarī commentary to that verse we see all Tantrayuktis, Tantraguṇas and Tantradoṣas being explained. The Tantradoṣas given there is presented below -

1. अप्रसिद्धशब्दम्- aprasiddhaśabdam - use words which are uncommon, unpopular or obselete.
2. दुष्प्रणीतम् - duṣpraṇītam - an ill-composed work (introduction, conclusion etc in disarray)
3. असङ्गतार्थम् - asaṅgatārtham -Not connected to the original theme or source text (if a commentary)
4. असुखारोहि(पदम्) - asukhārohi(padam) To use words that are hard to pronounce and therefore unpleasant to the ears.
5. विरुद्धम् - Viruddham – Opposed to convention, philosophy and logic
6. अतिविस्तृतम् - ativistṛtam – Very elaborate
7. अतिसङ्क्षिप्तम् - atisaṃkṣiptam - Very brief
8. अप्रयोजनम् – aprayojanam - Not mentioning utility
9. भिन्नक्रमम् – bhinnakramam - To not adhere to the serial order in which the items are mentioned previously even when there is no purpose to do so.
10. सन्दिग्धम् – sandigdham - ambiguous
11. पुनरुक्तम् – punaruktam – Repetition
12. निष्प्रमाणकम् - niṣpramāṇakam – Not based on evidence.
13. असमाप्तार्थम् – asamāptārtham – Incomplete

14. अनर्थकम् अथवा अपार्थकम् – apā(na)rthakam - Meaningless expressions or wrong meaning
15. व्याहतम् – vyāhatam – Self contradictory statements;

On analysing the points above it can be noted that these Tantradoṣas also point to flaws in

- Content: 3,5, 10- 13
- structure: 2, 8, 9,15
- language: 1,4,6,7, 14 - of a treatise

Tantraguṇa s and Tantradoṣas in Tamil Tradition

It is very interesting to note that even in the ancient Tamil literary tradition ten mistakes of a text and ten virtues of a text have been discussed. In the tamil treatise Nannul (13th Century CE) the beuties and faults of treatises are listed. A short exposition is given hereunder[171].

Ten Beauties of a treatise

1. சுருங்கச்சொல்லல் (Curungaccollal) - Brevity or conciseness
2. விளங்கவைத்தல் (Vilanga Vaittal) - Perspicuity or comprehensiveness
3. நவின்றோர்கினிமை (Navinrārkinimai) - agreeableness
4. நல் மொழி புணர்த்தல் (Nal Mozi Punarttal)- use of appropriate reputable words
5. ஓசையுடைமை (Ōcai Uḍaimai) - harmony or rhythm.
6. ஆழமுடைத்தாதல் - (Azamuaittātal) - profoundity of thought
7. முறையின்வைப்பு (Muraiyin Vaippu) - regularity of method
8. உலகம் மலையாமை (Ulagam Malaiyāmai) conformity with the opinions of the good and the great so as not to puzzle the world.

171 Ten beauties of a treatise (verse 13), Te Faults of a treatise (verse 12) Reference: naṉṉūl mūlamum viruttiyuraiyum, International Institute of Tamil Studies, Chennai, 1999 and The Nannul, Tamil text with English translation, Rev.H. Bower, pp.11-12

9. விழுமியது பயத்தல் - (Vizumiyatu Payattal) - sterling worthiness of subject matter
10. விளங்கு உதாரணத்து ஆகுதல் (Vilangu Utāranattu āgutal) - appropriate examples and illustration.

Ten Faults of a treatise

1. குன்றக்கூறல் (Kunaṛakkūṛal) - paucity of words
2. மிகைபடக்கூறல் (Migaipaḍakkūṛal) - prolixity
3. கூறியது கூறல் (Kūriyatu Kūral) tautology
4. மாறுகொளக்கூறல் (Māṛukoḷakkūṛal) - contradiction
5. வழூஉச்சொல் புணர்த்தல் (Vazuuccol Punarttal) - the use of incorrect or inappropriate words
6. மயங்கவைத்தல் (Mayangavaittal) - confusion or ambiguity
7. வெற்றெனத்தொடுத்தல் (Verrenattoḍuttal) -too great simplicty or unrefinedness
8. மற்றொறொன்று விரித்தல் (Marronru Virittal) -irrelevancey or far-fetchendness
9. சென்று தேய்ந்து இறுதல் (Ce<u>n</u><u>r</u>u tēyntu iruttal) unequalness
10. நின்று பயனின்மை (Ni<u>n</u><u>r</u>u paya<u>n</u>i<u>n</u>mai) unmeaningnes

It can be observed that these 10 faults and 10 beauties are found in the list of Saṃskṛta Tantraguṇa s and Tantradoṣas a few more mentioned in the Saṃskṛta tradition.

For easy comprehension the above list of Tantraguṇa s and Tantradoṣas can be summarized in the form of dos and donts in composing a treatise in content, structure and language

Which can be called as Bhāratiya Śodha Sāhitya Kṛtya-Akṛtya āvali. The checklist can be categorized into three sections: content, structure, and language. A tabulated version of the checklist is provided below.

CONTENT					
Kṛtya – Dos'			**Akṛtya Donts'**		
1	Comprehensive		1	Not connected to the original theme or source text	
2	Rich in meaning		2	Opposed to convention, philosophy and logic	
3	That which follows Rishi Tradition (preceeding wisdom)		3	Ambiguous	
4	Well evidenced		4	Repetitive	
5	Centered on Establishing facts		5	Not based on evidence	
			6	Incomplete	

Structure				
Kṛtya – Dos'			**Akṛtya Donts'**	
1	Non repetitive		1	Introduction, conclusion etc are in disarray
2	Follows briefing and elaboration systematically		2	Without statement of utility
3	Sequential		3	Self contradictory statements
4	Endowed with Logical flow		4	Repetitive
5	Without mixed up section		5	Non adherence to the serial order in which the items are mentioned previously

Language					
Kṛtya – Dos'			**Akṛtya Donts'**		
1	Appropriate words		1	Words which are uncommon, unpopular or archaic.
2	Easy words		2	Hard to pronounce words
3	Rich synonyms and descriptions		3	Very elaborate descriptions
4	Definitions		4	Very brief descrptions
5	Illustrations		5	Meaningless expressions or wrong meaning

The content in the tables above is self-explanatory.

Activities Based on Tantraguṇas & Tantradoṣa

Activity 1: Identification

1. **Dos and Don'ts Identification:**

   - **Question:** Read the following statements. Identify which ones are "dos" and which ones are "don'ts" in thesis writing.

     1. Start your thesis with a clear research question or hypothesis.
     2. Use informal language and slang.
     3. Cite all your sources accurately.
     4. Copy and paste text from other authors without citation.
     5. Proofread your thesis multiple times before submission.
     6. Rely solely on internet sources without checking their credibility.

Activity 2: Revision and Editing

2. **Revise the Paragraph:**

   - **Question:** Below is a poorly written paragraph from a thesis. Identify and correct the errors based on the dos and don'ts of thesis writing.

     "In my opinion, climate change is a big problem nowadays. There are many reasons for it, such as pollution and stuff.

Scientists says that if we don't do anything about it, things are gonna get worse. We should take actions now to stop this problem from becoming worse and destroying our planet."

- **Hint:** Look for issues related to tone, evidence, clarity, and citation.

Activity 3: Critical Thinking

3. **Evaluate Thesis Statements:**

   - **Question:** Evaluate the following thesis statements. Explain why each one is a strong or weak thesis statement.

     1. "This paper will discuss the impacts of climate change."
     2. "The industrial revolution had significant social and economic impacts on urbanization in the 19th century."
     3. "Some people think that exercise is good for health."
     4. "The rise of social media has dramatically altered communication patterns among teenagers."

Activity 4: Practical Application

4. **Create a Research Plan:**

   - **Question:** Develop a brief research plan for a thesis on the topic: "The effects of remote work on employee productivity." Outline your research question, potential sources, and a basic outline of chapters.

Activity 5: Peer Review

5. **Peer Review Simulation:**

   - **Question:** Pretend you are reviewing a peer's thesis draft. Here is an excerpt. Provide constructive feedback based on the dos and don'ts of thesis writing.

"The results of the experiment were amazing, showing a huge improvement in the subjects' memory after taking the supplement. However, we didn't really consider all the variables, so the results might not be 100% reliable."

Chapter 7

Closing Reflections & Opportunities for Advancement

In the preceeding chapters of this book - Tantrayuktis as a text/thesis construction methodology in various IKS domains was discussed with its functions, classical definitions and ample illustrations. Take aways for researchers and evaluators were also analytically presented with hands on activites for deeper engagement with Tantrayukits. Some closing observations on Tantrayuktis can be seen below that consolidates that content.

1. Tantrayuktis as Indigenous Methodology

Tantrayuktis, much like Bodhāyana's pre-Pythagorean version of the Pythagorean theorem, offers a time-tested, indigenous framework for thesis writing methodology that predates many non-indigenous approaches. Bhāratīya literature has long approached text construction and interpretation systematically, as evidenced by methodologies like Tantrayuktis, which reflect a structured and thoughtful tradition of intellectual inquiry. By adopting Tantrayuktis in research, we embrace a Svadeśī (self-reliant) methodology that fosters pride in India's rich intellectual heritage.

2. Ease of Integration, Promoting Bhāratīya Bhasha coherence

Tantrayuktis are deeply rooted in India's literary and scholarly traditions. This can be easily familized to Bhāratīya researchers, making it convenient for them to incorporate into their work compared to non-native methods. Resistance to research methods can also be reduced by adopting Tantrayuktis. Furthermore, as Tantrayuktis served as a common textual methodology across major linguistic traditions of Bharat, such as Saṃskṛta, Tamil, and Pāli, promoting Tantrayuktis can foster inter-linguistic studies within Bharat. This approach aligns with the vision of strengthening and encouraging the mutual interaction of Bhāratīya Bhashas, as outlined in the NEP 2020 document in numerous instances.

3. Compact, Direct and Flexible – thesis construction approach

Tantrayuktis offers a compact and accessible framework for thesis writing, with clear definitions and practical examples that make them easy to understand and apply. The content-structure-language approach - contribute to its straightforward nature, while its flexibility allows for adaptation, extension, or abridgment based on specific requirements (Refer: Customizable – Chapter 3). This quality makes it possible to integrate best practices from other text construction methodologies. It is important to note that Tantrayuktis is not presented as the sole approach to thesis writing; rather, it offers a dynamic template that complements other valuable research methods, both within Bharat and globally, fostering a well-rounded approach to research documentation

4. Integration into Mainstream in IKS and Non IKS domaions

This book not only highlights the historical significance of Tantrayuktis in Indian research traditions but also provides a practical framework for their application in contemporary research. While scholars have been aware of Tantrayuktis since the early 20th century (Refer: Definitions of Tantrayuktis, Chapter 1), its structured application in contemporary research has been long overdue. By proposing that every thesis, especially those in Saṃskṛtam (Sanskrit), include a dedicated section on Tantrayuktis, it ensures a systematic evaluation of content, structure, and language (C-S-L). This inclusion guides researchers and evaluators to adhere to high standards while maintaining the coherence and rigor of Indian textual traditions. Initially, Tantrayuktis can be introduced and applied within the domains of Indian Knowledge Systems (IKS), leveraging the deep-rooted frameworks already present in these traditions. Based on practical experience and with suitable customization, this approach can then be extended to non-IKS domains as well. This gradual integration allows for a tailored adaptation, ensuring that the systematic methodology of Tantrayuktis can contribute effectively across various fields of research.

5. Tantrayuktis as a tool for contemporary literary Criticism

Tantrayuktis, rooted in ancient textual methodologies, offers an innovative approach not only for evaluating classical texts but also for assessing contemporary content. By applying these principles to a wide spectrum of works—from popular literature to academic research across languages in Bharat and beyond—Tantrayuktis can serve as a versatile tool for textual analysis. Even in the realm of AI-based text evaluation, the devices of Tantrayuktis can be adapted to establish foundational criteria, ensuring a blend of traditional wisdom and modern technological advancement.

6. **Tantrayuktis as a means and an end**

However, while the current knowledge of Tantrayuktis is based on available sources, it is essential to continue strengthening research in this area. A renewed effort to mine the vast wealth of ancient Indian Knowledge Systems (IKS) texts will deepen the understanding of Tantrayuktis's presence and application. Based on that, its relevance in contemporary research practices within and beyond IKS can be broadened. It is impossible to realize the various promising outcomes from Tantrayuktis unless its source is thoroughly studied and data emerging form it is consolidated and organized into a useable document. The complete picture has to emerge. It can be stated that many textual research theses can be written on Tantrayuktis itself. Therefore, Tantrayuktis can serve both as a means for research by providng thesis writing tools and as the end goal or objective of the research itself.

7. Rediscovering lost Bridges

Jean-Luc Chevillard's (Chevillard 2009:71- 132) statement regarding Tantrayuktis is worth noting. He states -

> *"It is only by painstaking comparison of individual glosses for* Tantrayuktis *(*Tantrayuktis*) and TUS (Tantiravuttis), making extended use of...many other works... that one can hope to finally rediscover the lost bridges that have linked Tamil and Saṃskṛta technical literatures for a long time."*

(Chevillard 2009:117)

It is regrettable that the crucial dimension of the Tamil-Saṃskṛta connection, particularly in the context of Tantrayuktis, has been largely overlooked in both Saṃskṛta and Tamil academic spheres. It is very well known that the artificial socio-political divide created, cloud the relationship between Tamil and Saṃskṛta. Exploring Tamil-Saṃskṛta connect through Tantrayuktis becomes essential for rediscovering the lost bridges that once unified these traditions. Thus, this work is not just an academic exercise but a national imperative, as fostering this connection through textual studies holds the potential to strengthen the unity and integrity of Bharat.

To Conclude

एकस्मिन्नपि यस्येह शास्त्रे लब्धास्पदा मतिः
स शास्त्रमन्यदप्याशु युक्तिज्ञत्वात् प्रबुध्यते॥[172]

(Caraka-saṃhitā siddhisthāna 12.47-48)

(Based on the knowledge of the Yuktis*) The one whose mind has gained foothold in one śāstra (discipline of knowledge), can quickly grasp other śāstra-s as well as he is a Yuktijña (the one who aware of the* Yuktis *or methodology)*

---

172 ekasminnapi yasyeha śāstre labdhāspadā matiḥ
sa śāstramanyadapyāśu yuktijñatvāt prabudhyate..

Had this statement of Caraka been taken seriously long ago, Tantrayuktis would have become an integral part of research methodology courses for research studies across disciplines. They could also have been used as a tool for evaluating theses. As the saying goes, better late than never; it is essential to address this need now.

Furthermore, in this era of renewed interest in Indian Knowledge Systems, it is crucial to develop a comprehensive and robust methodology for these systems. This work on Tantrayuktis represents a humble step in this direction. Strengthening and expanding this foundation is essential for consolidating and fortifying the methodological underpinnings of studies in Indian Knowledge Systems.

Appendix 1

30 Minutes Talk & 3 Hours Lecture on Tantrayuktis

30 Minute IIT Talk

Scan QR code to listen to a 30 mintue lecture on the topic "Rediscovering the Lost Bridges: Tantrayuktis - Taṇṭiravutti, An Ancient Pan-Indian, Trans-lingual Text-construction Manual" by Prof M Jayaraman at IIT Madras, in the Swadeshi Indology Conference – 3, 22nd-24th of December 2017.

3 Hour University Lecture with Q &A

Scan QR Code to a listen to lecture on "Tantrayuktis *Devices to Refine Content, Structure and Language of a Thesis* by Prof. M Jayaraman (of duration 2:54:02). This lecture was hosted by Department of Saṃskṛta Studies, University of Hyderabad. It was a national workshop on Bhāratīya Anusandhāna Paddhati (Indian Research Methodology), November 15-18, 2023

Appendix 2

The Tolkāppiyam List and Defitions of Tantiravuttis

Previously Saṃskṛta Tantrayuktis from the Arthaśāstra were discussed. Here is the list of Tantiravuttis from the Tolkāppiyam (Mararpiyal Porulatikāram, Sūtra 665) along with their definitions translated from Tamil lexicons, dictionaries, and commentaries.

1. *Nuṭaliyatu arital* - A literary device that consists in stating ones theme before dealing with it in detail. (Gopaliyyer, 2005 Vol 16:308)[173]*atikāramuraiye* - The logical order of subjects in a book. (Gopaliyyer, 2005, Vol 1:73)
2. *tokuttukkūral* - A literary device that assists in summarizing / abridgement in a statement of what is to be stated in detail. (Gopaliyyer, 2005, Vol 16 2005:297)
3. *vakuttu meyniruttal* - Defining concepts in detail that were stated in sets. (Gopaliyyer, 2005 Vol 16:362)
4. *molinta poruḷoṭonravavvayin moliyātatanai muṭṭinri muṭittal* - a) When the text yields scope for several meanings, deciding upon one meaning in consonance with the earlier portion of the text. b) When the author does not explicitly state the meaning of a particular term, deciding upon a meaning with the help of a secondary text. 2) Adding a an apt but unstated view that fits into the topic under discussion. (Gopaliyyer, 2005, Vol 16:362)

173 Gopaliyyer, T. V. (2005). Tamiz llakkaṇa Pēragarāti Volumes 1-17 Chennai: Tamiz Man Publishers.

5. *vārātataṉai vaṉtu muṭittal* - A literary device by which the sense of Sūtra insufficiently expressed is rendered complete. (Gopaliyyer, 2005 Vol 16:371)

6. *vaṉtatu koṇṭu varātatu uṇarttal* – A literary device which consists in applying to an earlier statement an implication drawn from a later explicit statement. (Tamil Lexicon, Vol. 6: 3490)[174]

7. *Muṉṟu muṭintatu talai taṭumāṟṟe* - Establishing an idea by reversing the order of a list of concepts stated already. (Gopaliyyer, 2005, Vol 6:3490)

8. *oppakkūṟal* - Defining a concept in such a way that allows the applicability of the definition to its parts too. (Gopaliyyer 2005, Vol 16:359)

9. *oru talai moḻital* - Stating that a defintion metioned elsewhere in the text should be applied to the present context also. (Gopaliyyer, 2005, Vol 16:244)

10. *taṉ koḷ kūṟal* - Emphasizing ones own view, though there may be many views, regarding a concept. (Gopaliyyer 2005, Vol 16:290)

11. *muṟai piṟaḻāmai* - Describing concepts in the order of enumeration committed earlier and in consonance with the earlier stated view. (Gopaliyyer, 2005, Vol 16:329)

12. *piṟar uṭaṉ paṭṭatu tāṉ uṭaṉ paṭutal* -Accepting the view of other authors views as they are. (Gopaliyyer, 2005, Vol 16:222)

13. *iṟantatu kāttal* - 1) If an idea is not clearly expressed in one occasion explaining the same later in some other context. 2) Refuting the view stated earlier in the text in a later occasion. 3) Not contradicting a rule stated earlier if it had to be repeated elsewhere. 4) Removing archaic language, meaning and conventions from the text. (Vellaivaranar 1994: 202,221)[175]

---

174 Tamil Lexicon, Volumes I to VI, (1982), Published Under the Authority of University of Madras, Madras

175 Vellaivaranar (1994) Tolkāppiyam marapiyal uraivaḻam, Publication Division Madurai, Kāmaraj University, Maudrai

14. *etiratu poṟṟal* - Updation of the revision of an earlier concept. (Gopaliyyer, 2005, Vol 16:363)
15. *moḻivām eṉṟal* - Stating that a concept would be treated later in the text. (Gopaliyyer, 2005, Vol 16:266)
16. *kūṟiṟṟeṉṟal* - Pointing out that in a previous instance in the text a specific definition has been stated. (Tamil Lexicon Vol5. 1982:1858)
17. *tāṉ kuṟiyiṭutal* - Following one's own terminology in one's work. (Gopaliyyer, 2005, Vol 16: 243)
18. *orutalaiyaṉmai* - A literary device that assists in stating the possibility of an alternative interpretation to a present concept that is being defined. (Gopaliyyer, 2005, Vol 16:355)
19. *muṭintatu kāṭṭal* - Rather than explaining all the aspects of a concept at hand just referring to an earlier author's view regarding the concept. (Gopaliyyer, 2005, Vol 16:212-213)
20. āṇai *kūṟal* - Stating a rule through injunction without adducing a reason. (Gopaliyyer, 2005, Vol 16:323)
21. *pal poruṭku eṟpiṉ nallatu koṭal* - Fixing the best meaning among them that suits the context If a word phrase or sentence seems to yield multiple meanings. (Tamil Lexicon Vol5. 1982:2078)
22. *tokuttu moḻiyāṉ vakuttatu koṭal* - The literary device of stating by a general term what is described in detail under various heads. (Gopaliyyer, 2005, Vol 16:350)
23. *maṟu talai citaittu taṉ tuṇipuraittal* -Refuting the views of others with proper proofs and establishing one's own view. (Tamil Lexicon Vol5. 1982:2721)
24. *piṟaṉ koḷ kūṟal* - Quoting the opinion of others. (Gopaliyyer, 2005, Vol 16:340)
25. *aṟiyātu uṭampaṭal* - Accepting a concept stated by others, which is unknown to oneself. (Vellaivaranar 1994:229)
26. *poruḷ iṭaimiṭutal* - Showing that a definition spelled out pertains to a particular word with a certain meaning. (Gopaliyyer, 2005, Vol 16:237)

27. *etirporuḷuṇarttal* - Keeping in view the future changes in mind while defining a particular concept. (Gopaliyyer, 2005, Vol 16:284)
28. *collin̲ eccam colliyāṅku uṇarttal* - Indicating certain ideas through implication rather than explicitly stating them. (Gopaliyyer, 2005, Vol 16:287)
29. *Tan̲tu puṇarntu uraittal* - Bringing an idea expressed earlier or later to a place where it fits the context. (Tamil Lexicon Vol3. 1982:1685)
30. ñāpakam *kūr̲al* - An art where by the full content of a sūtra is merely indicated in general terms. (Tamil Lexicon Vol1. 1982:433)
31. *uyttukkoṇṭuṇarttal* - A literary method consisting in the use in an exposition of such expression as would stimulate thought or further enquiry. (Vellaivaranar 1994:232)

At the end of the enumeration of the *Utti*-s, *Tolkāppiyam* states that similar to that of the 32 *Utti*-s many more can also be added and they should be accommodated (with in the 32) and appropriately treated. (*Tolkāppiyam Sūtra 665*).

Appendix 3

Comparitive Table of Tantrayuktis in Various Saṃskṛta Treatises

SNo	AS	CS	SS	VDP	YD
1	adhikaraṇam	adhikaraṇam	adhikaraṇam	adhikaraṇam	sūtropapattiḥ
2	vidhānam	yogaḥ	yogaḥ	yogaḥ	pramāṇopapattiḥ
3	yogaḥ	hetvartha	padārthaḥ	padārthaḥ	avayavopapattiḥ
4	padārthaḥ	padārthaḥ	hetvārtha:	hetvarthaḥ	anyūnatā
5	hetvarthaḥ	pradeśa:	uddeśaḥ	uddeśaḥ	saṃśayanirṇayoktiḥ
6	uddeśaḥ	uddeśaḥ	nirdeśa:	nirdeśaḥ	uddeśanirdeśam
7	nirdeśaḥ	nirdeśa:	upadeśa:	upadeśaḥ	anukramaḥ
8	upadeśaḥ	vākyaśeṣaḥ	apadeśaḥ	apadeśaḥ	saṃjñā
9	apadeśaḥ	prayojanam	pradeśaḥ	pradeśaḥ	upadeśaḥ
10	atideśaḥ	upadeśaḥ	atideśaḥ	atideśaḥ	
11	pradeśaḥ	apadeśaḥ	apavargaḥ	apavargaḥ	
12	upamānam	atideśaḥ	vākyaśeṣaḥ	vākyaśeṣaḥ	
13	arthāpattiḥ	arthāpattiḥ	arthāpattiḥ	arthāpattiḥ	
14	saṃśayaḥ	nirṇayaḥ	viparyayaḥ	prasaṅgaḥ	
15	prasaṅgaḥ	prasaṅgaḥ	prasaṅgaḥ	ekāntaḥ	
16	viparyayaḥ	ekānta:	ekāntaḥ	anaikāntaḥ	
17	vākyaśeṣaḥ	naikantaḥ	anekāntaḥ	pūrvapakṣa:	
18	anumatam	apavargaḥ	pūrvapakṣa:	nirṇayaḥ	
19	vyākhyānam	viparyayaḥ	nirṇaya:	vidhānam	
20	nirvacanam	pūrvapakṣa:	anumatam	viparyayaḥ	
21	nidarśanam	vidhānama	vidhānam	atikrāntāvekṣaṇam	
22	apavargaḥ	anumatam	anāgatāvekṣaṇam	anāgatāvekṣaṇam	
23	svasaṃjñā	vyākhyānam	atikrāntāvekṣaṇam	saṃśayaḥ	
24	pūrvapakṣaḥ	saṃśayaḥ	saṃśayaḥ	ativyākhyānam	
25	uttarapakṣaḥ	atītāvekṣā	vyakhyānam	anumatam	

26	ekāntaḥ	anāgatāvekṣā / anāgatāpekṣā	svasaṃjñā	svasaṃjñā	
27	anāgatāvekṣaṇam	svasaṃjñā	nirvacanam	nirvacanam	
28	atikrāntāvekṣaṇam	ūhyam	nidarśanam	dṛṣṭāntaḥ	
29	niyogaḥ	samuccayaḥ	niyogaḥ	niyogaḥ	
30	vikalpaḥ	nidarśanam	vikalpaḥ	vikalpaḥ	
31	samuccayaḥ	nirvacanam	samuccyaḥ	samuccayaḥ	
32	ūhyam	sanniyogaḥ/ niyogaḥ	ūhyam	ūhyam	
33	-	vikalpanam			
34	-	pratyutsāraḥ			
35	-	uddhāraḥ			
36	-	sambhavaḥ			

AS – Arthaśāstra | CS – Caraka-saṃhitā | SS Suśruta-saṃhitā | VDP – Viṣṇudharmottarapurāṇa | YD – Yuktidīpikā

Appendix 4

Comparitive Table of Yuktis of Kauṭilya

Arthaśāstra and Tolkāppiyam

S.No	Yukti of Arthaśāstra	Yukti of Tolkāppiyam
1	atikrāntāvekṣaṇam	Kūrirrenral
2	adhikaraṇam	Nutaliyarital
3	anumatam	Piranuḍambaṭṭatu Tānuḍampaḍutal
4	apadeśaḥ	Piran Kōḷkūṛal
5	arthāpattiḥ	Mo̱linta poruḷoṭu o̱ṉ̱ravavvaiyiṉ Mo̱liyātatanai Muṭṭiṉ̱ṟi Muḍittal
6	uttarapakṣaḥ	Maṛutalaicitaittu Taṉṟuṇipuraittal
7	uddeśaḥ	Toguttukkūṛal
8	ūhyam	Uyttukkonduṇarttal
9	niyogāḥ	Āṇaikūṛal
10	nirvacanam	Porulidaiyiḍutal
11	vikalpaḥ	Palporutkērpin Nallatu Kōḍal
12	vidhānam	Atikāramuraimai
13	viparyayaḥ	Muṉ̱ṟu mo̱linta tāṉ Talaitaḍumārrē
14	saṃśayaḥ	oru talayanmai
15	svasaṃjñā	Tankuriyiḍutal

Reference: Jayaraman, M. (2009), The Doctrine of Tantrayuktis – A Study, Ph.D. thesis Submitted to the University of Madras, p.238

Appendix 5

50 Questions for Assesment

These 50 questions can be used to review your study of the book. Alternatively, if you have opened the book from this section you can start reading the book from here also. If you know answers to all these questions. There is no need to go into the book. You can gift it to other. If you do not know, explore the various chapters herein and find the answers.

1. According to SC Vidyabhushana what is the period of compilation of Tantrayuktis?

   a) 6th Century BCE
   b) 6th Century CE
   c) 16th Century BCE
   d) 16th Century CE

2. Which is the oldest known text to have dealt with Tantrayuktis in a full-fledged manner?

   a) nyāyasūtrabhāṣya
   b) Viṣṇudharmottarapurāṇa
   c) Arthaśāstra
   d) Tantrayuktisvicāra

3. Select the two texts of **Āyurveda** that have utilized Tantrayuktis

   a) Yuktidīpikā & Caraka-saṃhitā
   b) Caraka-saṃhitā & Suśrutasaṃhitā

c) Suśrutasaṃhitā & Arthaśāstra
d) Nyāyasūtrabhāśya & Caraka-saṃhitā

4. What is the meaning of Tantra in the term Tantrayuktis?

a) Āyurveda
b) Definition
c) A system of Spiritual practice
d) A Discipline of knowledge

5. Which among the below are not among the three major components of Tantrayuktis.

a) Tantraśāstra
b) Tantradoṣa
c) Tantrayuktis
d) Tantraguṇa

6. Number of Yuktis have been defined and Illustrated in Arthaśāstra

a) 33
b) 23
c) 32
d) 36

7. The number of Tantraguṇas and Tantradoṣas are ____ & ______ respectively.

a) 15 & 16
b) 15 & 19
c) 19 & 15
d) 16 & 19

8. What are the Indic textual-literary traditions that have evidences and indications towards the utilization of Tantrayuktis?

a) Saṃskṛta, Gujarati, Pāli
b) Tamil, Saṃskṛta, Malayalam

c) Telugu, Tamil, Kannada
d) Saṃskṛta, Tamil and Pāli

9. The three areas with regard to thesis construction to which Tantrayuktis contribute are:

a) Content, Structure, Inference
b) Content, Structure, Language
c) Language, Data, Analysis
d) Language, Analysis, structure

10. Restricting a pervasive Rules is ________ Yukti

a) uttarapakṣa
b) vidhāna
c) ūhya
d) apavarga

11. Referring to a statement by another author is ________ Yukti.

a) apadeśa
b) upamāna
c) pūrvapakṣa
d) upadeśa

12. Combining homogenous ideas and stating them together is ________Yukti

a) arthāpattiḥ
b) prasaṅgaḥ
c) samuccayaḥ
d) yogaḥ

13. Cogently connecting the words in a sentence is ________ Yukti.

a) anumata
b) yoga

c) svasaṃjñā
d) ekānta

14. Adhikaraṇa refers to the statement of ______________ of the treatise.

a) Subject matter
b) Limitations
c) Methodology
d) Conclusion

15. Nirdeśa Yuktis Pairs with which Yuktis ________________.

a) pradeśa
b) uddeśa
c) apadeśa
d) vākyaśeṣa

16. **āyurvidyate** asmin, anena vā **āyurvindatīti** – *that in which **āyus** – discussion on extending life span is found, or that by which **āyus** is attained is called **āyurveda*** - What is the Yuktis being illustrated here?

a) Nidarśana (example)
b) vyākhyāna (explanation)
c) padārtha (contextual meaning)
d) nirvacana (etymological derivation)

17. *"Do not eat curds during night, or without ghee or sugar"* – this means one can eat curds in day time – Find the Yuktis illustrated here.

a) Nidarśanam (example)
b) arthāpattiḥ (implication)
c) padārthaḥ (contextual meaning)
d) nirvacanam (etymological derivation)

18. Thirteen types of treatment by Sveda(sweating/sudation therapy) has been stated in chapter on Sveda" - This statement is in 6th chapter on Jvara - fever. The Sveda section is found in the 1st chapter. What is the Yuktis used here?

    a) atikrantāvekṣaṇa (reference to a past elaboration)
    b) anāgatāvekṣaṇa (reference to a future elaboration)
    c) pradeśa (applying rule to be stated later to the present context)
    d) atideśaḥ (applying a rule stated earlier to the present context)

19. *"The wise physician should eliminate or exclude the drugs if it is not appropriate even if enumerated under the group and should add the appropriate one even if un-enumerated. If required, a group of drugs may be combined with other or several other groups based on the reasoning."*. Which Yuktis is illustrated here?

    a) Nidarśana (example)
    b) atideśa (applying a rule stated earlier to the present context)
    c) ūhya (rules that require context conscious application)
    d) saṃśaya (doubt)

20. Find out that set of Yuktis that are not connected by a theme:

    a) upadeśa, apadeśa, pradeśaḥ atideśaḥ
    b) uddeśa nirdeśa, pradeśaḥ atideśaḥ
    c) vikalpa hetvārtha saṃśaya anumatam
    d) svasaṃjñā, nirvacana, vyākhyāna, vākyaśeṣaḥ

21. From the bunch of 15 Yuktis below, classify them correctly under the three heads - Content, structure and language

    yoga, uttarapakṣa, upadeśa, uddeśa, vākyaśeṣa, viparyaya, pradeśa, adhikaraṇa, ekānta, niyoga, arthāpātti, ūhya, nirvacana, apadeśa, padārtha

22. Find the odd Yuktis out

    a) adhikaraṇa, vidhāna, viparyaya, saṃśaya
    b) padārtha, vākyaśeṣa, yoga, pūrvapakṣa
    c) upadeśa, apadeśa, ūhya. vikalpa
    d) vikalpa hetvārtha saṃśaya nirdeśa
    e) svasaṃjñā, nirvacana, vyākhyāna, anumata

23. Match the Following Yuktis with their meanings

1.	saṃśaya	Exception to a rule
2.	anumatam	advice/suggestion
3.	upadeśa	prima facie view/view to be rejected
4.	pūrvapakṣa	invent new terminology
5.	svasaṃjñā	Explain
6.	vyākhyāna	reference to a past classification
7.	apavarga	extending the application of a rule discussed earlier to the current context
8.	vidhāna	quoting and accepting others views
9.	atikrātāvekṣaṇa	Table of content
10.	atideśa	an issue with two valid sides/causes

24. How does Lele introduce Tantrayuktis methodology? Mention any 5 aspects.
25. Quote the views of atleast 5 scholars about Tantrayuktis
26. Discuss the meaning of the terms Tantra and Yuktis which are part of the compound term Tantrayuktis.
27. What are the three ways in which Tantrayuktis have been utilized in texts?
28. As per available literary evidences, what are the disciplines that have utilized the methodology of Tantrayuktis?
29. Briefly discuss the Lamp and Sunlight example that present the function of Tantrayuktis.
30. Write a note on the functions of Tantrayuktis as per Suśruta.
31. How do we know that Tantrayuktis was meant to be a methodology document?

32. Should all the 32 Tantrayuktis be utilized in all texts? Justify your answer.
33. Write a short note on the utilization of Tantrayuktis methodology in Non-Saṃskṛta literary traditions.
34. What do NE Muthuswamy and Esther Solomon state about the functions of Tantrayuktis?
35. Define Illustrate and Explain the following Yuktis

    a) viparyaya
    b) vidhāna
    c) anāgatāvekṣaṇa
    d) ūhya
    e) vikalpa

36. What Yuktis does the title of the books/articles suggest identify and Justify your answer –

    a) śāstras through the lens of Western Indology – A Response, Ed.K.S. Kannan, Infinity Foundation, 2018
    b) Gunde Rao Harkare, "In defence of Yoga philosophy", PAIOC 19, 1955, 460-463
    c) Collective Defense Or Strategic Independence?: - Ted Galen Carpenter – 1989
    d) How to Give Effective Feedback to Your Students - Susan M. Brookhart – 2008

37. Discuss In detail the definitions and derivations (ancient and recent) of the term Tantrayuktis
38. Write an essay about the history of utilization of Tantrayuktis in Various texts.
39. Write an essay about the functions of Tantrayuktis as discussed by ancient texts and recent scholars.
40. Discuss the Yuktis with appropriate examples that help in developing the content of a thesis
41. Discuss the Yuktis with appropriate examples that help in developing the structure of a thesis

42. Discuss the Yuktis with appropriate examples that help in developing the language of a thesis
43. Discuss the inputs from the Tantraguṇa s and Tantradoṣas – on Content, Structure and Language of a thesis.
44. What are Tantrayuktis – of which the goodness or errors are pointed out by Tantraguṇa s and Tantradoṣas. Analyze.
45. Read the book review - https://www.academia.edu/4211123/Review_of_Yogi_Heroes_and_Poets

    Identify the Tantraguṇa s and Tantradoṣas. Or any other observations on Tantrayuktis devices. Quote appropriate statements from the review to substantiate your views.

46. Why do you think Tantrayuktis, despite their historical significance and widespread use in ancient Indian literary traditions, have not been integrated into modern research methodologies until now? What factors might have contributed to this oversight?
47. How can the study and comparison of Tantrayuktis in Saṃskṛta, Tamil, and Pāli texts contribute to a better understanding of the interconnectedness and unique features of these literary traditions? What methodological challenges might arise in such a comparative study?
48. Considering the diversity and variation in the list of Tantrayuktis across different texts and traditions, how can a standardized methodology be developed for modern academic use? What steps should be taken to ensure the effective integration of Tantrayuktis into contemporary research frameworks?
49. Based on the unresolved issues and scope for further work outlined in the text, what specific research projects or initiatives would you propose to advance the study and application of Tantrayuktis in Indian Knowledge Systems? How can interdisciplinary approaches enhance the research on Tantrayuktis?

50. Write a 2000 word article on topic of your choice (in Saṃskṛta, English or Hindi) and try to consciously incorporate as many Yuktis possible as applicable (do not try to insert extraneous Yuktis). Highlight the Yuktis that you have employed in your write up.

Appendix 6

References

1. Arthaśāstra See (Shamashastrary, R). (1915)
2. Āyurvedadīpikā, http://niimh.nic.in/ebooks/ecaraka/?mod=read, Accessed on September 3, 2017: E-book: Searchable: e-Book on 'Caraka-saṁhitā' with Āyurvēdadīpikā commentary of Cakrapāṇidatta, Developed by Central Council for Research in Āyurveda and Siddha (CCRAS), New Delhi.
3. Bhagavati, Dr.K., (1981), Tolkappiya Uraivalam, Porulatikaram, Mararpiyal, International Institute of Tamilstudies, Chennai
4. Caraka-saṃhitā, See Āyurvedadīpikā (2017)
5. Chevillard, Jean-Luc, 2009b, "The Metagrammatical Vocabulary inside the Lists of 32 Tantrayuktis and its Adaptation to Tamil: Towards a Saṃskṛta-Tamil Dictionary", pp. 71-132, in Wilden, Eva (Ed.), Between Preservation and Recreation: Proceedings of a workshop in honour of T.V. Gopal Iyer, Collection Indologie – 109, IFP/EFEO, Pondicherry.
6. Dalal, M.C & Sastri, Pandit R.A, (1934), Kāvyamīmāmsā Rājaśekhara, Oriental Institute, baroda
7. Das, Keshav Chandra (1992), Elements of Research Methodology in Saṃskṛta, Chaukhamba Saṃskṛta Sansthan, New Delhi.
8. Dishitar, V.R.Ramchandra, (1930), "Tantrayuktis" The Journal of Oriental Research, Kuppuswami Shastri Research Institute, Chennai, Vol.4, pp.82-91

9. Gopala Iyer, T.V (2005), Tamiz ilakkaṇa peragarāti, Volumes 1-16, Tamizh man Pathippagam (Publishers), Chennai
10. Iyer, V.Duraiswamy (1935), Tolkāppiya Porulatikāram, Part 2,, Sadhu Printers, Royapettah, Chennai
11. Jayaraman, M. (2009), The Doctrine of Tantrayuktis – A Study, Ph.D. thesis Submitted to the University of Madras
12. Kaul, Madhusudan (1921-35), Svacchanda Tantra with the Udyota of Kṣemarāja, 7 Volumes, Government Press, Srinagar
13. Kāvyamīmāmsā See (Dalal & Sastri) (1934)
14. Lele, Dr. W.K (1981), The Doctrine of Tantrayuktis, Chaukhamba Surabharati Prakāśan, Varanasi
15. Mittal, Surendra Nath, (2000), Kauṭilya Arthaśāstra Revisited, PHISPC, New Delhi
16. Muraleemadhavan, P.C. & Sundareswaran, K. (2006), Saṃskṛta in Technological Age, New Bharatiya Book Corporation, New Delhi.
17. Muthuswamy, N.E., (1974), Tantrayuktisvicāra, Publication Division, Government Āyurveda College, Trivandrum.
18. Narayan Ram, Acharya Kavya Tirtha (1945) Suśrutasaṃhitā, Nirnaya Sagar Press, Bombay
19. Nyāyasūtrabhāśyam See (Tailanga) (1896)
20. Obberhammer, Gerhard (1968), "Notes on Tantrayuktis", The Adyar Library Bulletin, Vol. 31, pp.600-611
21. Pandeya, Ram Chandra (1967), Yuktidīpikā, Motilal Banarsidas, New Delhi
22. Regular Courses available in Āyurveda, http://ayush.gov.in/sites/default/files/6729652177-Regular%20Courses%20available%20in%20Āyurveda_0.pdf, Accessed on September 2, 2017.
23. Raghavaiyengar, Ra. (1952) Tamiḻ varalāṟu, Annamalai University, Annamalai Nagar (pp.297-324)
24. Sastri, Vempaṭi Kuṭumba & Sarma, K. V. (2002), Science texts in Saṃskṛta in the Manuscripts repositories of Kerala and Tamilnadu, Rashtriya Saṃskṛta Sansthan, New Delhi

25. Sastri, M.K (1945), Vamakeśvarīmatavivaraṇam, Research Department, Jammu and Kashmir State, Srinagar.
26. Sastri, P.S.Subrahmanya (1946), An Enquiry into the Relationship of Saṃskṛta and Tamil, University of Travnacore, Trivandrum.
27. Shamashastrary, R. (1915), Arthaśāstra, Government press, Bangalore
28. Sharma, śaṅkara (1949), Tantrayuktis, Vaidyasarathi Press, Kottayam
29. Sharma, K.V (2006) Science of Ancient India: Certain Novel Facets In Their Study, Dr.K.V.Sharma p.31-32 See (Muraleemadhavan, P.C. & Sundareswaran), K. (2006)
30. Shastri, Mukunda Ram (1942), The īIśvarapratyabhijñāvivṛ tivimarśinī of Abhinavagupta, Nirnayasagar, Bombay
31. Sengupta, Kaviraja Narendranath, Sengupta, Kaviaraja Balaichandra (1933), Caraka-saṃhitā carakacaturānana śrīmacCakrapāṇidattapraṇītayā Āyurvedadīpikākhyaṭīkayā mahāmahopādhyāya śrīgaṅgādharakaviratnavirājaviracitayā jalpakalpatarusamākhyayā ṭīkayā ca samalaṅkṛtā, CK Sen and Company, Kolkatta
32. Solomon, Esther (1978), Indian Dialectics: Methods of Philosophical Discussions, B.J.Institute of Learning and research, Ahmedabad.
33. Svacchandatantra see Kaul, Madhusudan (1921-35)
34. Suśrutasaṃhitā see (Narayan Ram, Acharya Kavya Tirtha) (1945)
35. Tailanga, Gangadhara Shastri (1896), Nyayasūtras with Vātsyāyana Bhāṣya, E.J.Lazarus & company, Benares
36. Tamil Lexicon, Volumes I to VI, (1982), Published Under the Authority of University of Madras, Madras.
37. Tolkāppiyam See (Iyer, V.Duraiswamy) (1935)
38. Vamakeśvarīmatavivaraṇam See Sastri, M.K (1945)
39. Vellaivaranar (1994) Tolkāppiyam mararpiyal uraivaḻam, Publication Division Madurai, Kāmaraj University, Maudrai

40. Vidyabhushana, Dr. Satis Chandra (1921), A History of Indian Logic, Motilal Banarsidas, Calcutta
41. Wardner, A.K, (1998) Indian Buddhism, Moitilal Banarsidas, New Delhi

www.ingramcontent.com/pod-product-compliance
Lightning Source LLC
Chambersburg PA
CBHW030009290326
41934CB00005B/275
* 9 7 8 1 9 7 0 4 5 2 0 0 6 *